Not Just Numbers

Examining the Legitimacy
of Foreign Debts

Edited by Martin Junge and Peter N. Prove
in collaboration with Frederick Schlagenhaft

on behalf of

The Lutheran World Federation –
A Communion of Churches

Lutheran University Press
Minneapolis, Minnesota

Not Just Numbers.
Examining the Legitimacy of Foreign Debts
Documentation No. 53, October 2008

Martin Junge and Peter N. Prove, editors
in collaboration with Frederick Schlagenhaft
on behalf of The Lutheran World Federation – A Communion of Churches

Translators: Anthony Coates, Nathan Lechler, Margaret Pater
Editorial assistance: LWF Office for Communication Services
Design: LWF-OCS
Cover: numbers by Thomas Hawk / thomashawk.com, faces © Nathalie Pahud-Briquet

Published by Lutheran University Press under the auspices of:
The Lutheran World Federation
150, rte de Ferney, PO Box 2100
CH-1211 Geneva 2, Switzerland

Parallel edition in German available from Kreuz Verlag, Stuttgart, Germany
"Nicht nur Zahlen. Kritische Fragen zur Legitimität von Auslandsschulden"

This book is also available in Europe under ISBN 978-3-905676-66-2.

Library of Congress Cataloging-in-Publication Data

Not just numbers : examining the legitimacy of foreign debts / Martin Junge and Peter N. Prove, editors ; in collaboration with Frederick Schlagenhaft.
    p. cm. — (Documentation ; no. 53)
  ISBN-13: 978-1-932688-37-5 (alk. paper)
  ISBN-10: 1-932688-37-4 (alk. paper)
  1. Debts, External—Developing countries. 2. Debts, External—Religious aspects—Christianity. 3. International finance—Moral and ethical aspects. I. Junge, Martin. II. Prove, Peter N.
  HJ8899.N675 2008
  336.3'435091724—dc22

                 2008041348

Lutheran University Press, PO Box 390759, Minneapolis, MN 55439
Manufactured in the United States of America

Contents

Preface

Debt is not just a matter of economics. It is something that implicates and often deeply affects relationships, whether between individuals or between states. A debt relationship must be based upon transparency, voluntariness, and trust and mutuality between lender and borrower. But a debt arrangement that is unjust, corrupt or oppressive, or lacks mutuality, is deeply corrosive, not only of the relationship but of each of the parties involved. When such an arrangement takes away the strength of one party, it undermines the moral strength of both.

Debt therefore comprises both a material and a spiritual dimension. It is accordingly an appropriate matter to revisit from the perspective of ethics and justice. The Lutheran World Federation has established its program on illegitimate debt in order to examine the problem of debt from this perspective and to encourage others, including governments, to do likewise.

The Lutheran World Federation has welcomed the initiatives of such governments as those of Norway and Ecuador in taking concrete steps to analyze and deal with sovereign debt crises from the perspective of legitimacy or illegitimacy. Beyond such isolated initiatives, we believe that cases of injustice in sovereign debt relationships need a systemic response adapted to dealing with and resolving each such case.

Such a response is in the interests of both debtor and creditor. When Norway unilaterally cancelled debts arising from its discredited ship export campaign, it recognized both its moral responsibility to the people of the debtor countries and the moral damage Norway itself had sustained. In cancelling these debts, it acted appropriately not only for the sake of the people of the debtor countries, but for its own sake.

Through this publication, the Lutheran World Federation seeks to lift up such examples and the experiences and insights of churches and their partners in the fields of politics, academia and civil society. We invite you, in reading these pages, to re-examine and reflect on debt from the perspective of justice and legitimacy, to focus on both the moral and spiritual dimensions of debt relationships, and to consider the damage that illegitimate debts do to both parties. And then join us in demanding the establishment of a justice-driven response to the continuing debt crisis.

In this task, may we all be inspired by the recognition that it is not just numbers of which we speak, but justice, dignity, hope and life.

Rev. Dr Ishmael Noko
General Secretary, The Lutheran World Federation

Foreword

Kjell Nordstokke

Many years ago I heard Archbishop Helder Camara telling about a meeting with a group of poor farmers in north-eastern Brazil. On that occasion he spoke to them about their country's enormous foreign debt and how much each of them would owe if the whole debt were to be distributed equally among all citizens. The audience at first became very silent as they realized that their share of the debt was far beyond what they could possibly earn throughout their entire lives. Then one man stood up and said, "But we are honest and decent people. What we borrow, we always pay back!"

This simple story illustrates the profound dilemma of honest, hard-working, poor people in the global South, trapped in an environment of indebtedness where they carry the costs while never benefitting from the money that was borrowed. But they do indeed pay their share, as indebted poor countries are obliged to reduce governmental support toward education, health and social services. The poorest sectors of society are always struck hardest by these measures.

Such a reality already clearly depicts the moral dilemma of international debt. Its immoral nature becomes even more obvious as there is proof that significant portions of the debt are contracted under dubious circumstances and without basic respect for legal rules and procedures. Deals are concluded in closed rooms, decisions are made by persons lacking democratic support, and information about lending conditions is kept secret.

The issue of illegitimate debt, as it is raised in Latin America by member churches of the Lutheran World Federation, has this moral aspect as its starting point. The question is not whether borrowed money will be paid back. The Latin American church leaders share the position of all honest, decent people, as shown by the story from north-eastern Brazil. But if the illegitimacy of the debt can be documented, then things become different. Why should poor people pay for what some smart people have arranged owing to their position and ability to manipulate for their own interest and not for the well-being of the people?

Beyond this obvious ethical issue, the Latin American church leaders also pointed out another dimension, an existential one. In their own congregations they experience growing poverty, which not only sets people back economically and socially, but also affects their self-esteem and dignity as human beings. This experience prompted them to raise the following questions: How does this reality impact the life and the mission of the church? How do we interpret the biblical message of human dignity in such a context? How do we announce the good news of justification in Christ when everyday life proclaims injustice?

Wrestling with such questions, the theological dimension of the matter became prominent. The churches realized that they were called upon to speak up against illegitimate debt, and to do so publicly—consciously—as churches, in God's name and in the name of all voiceless people.

But they also realized that most of the Lutheran churches in Latin America are small and rather unknown in the public sphere. This fact made evident that their action would have to be taken in communion and with the support of international partners. When Lutheran church leaders met at their annual regional leadership conference in Santa Cruz, Bolivia, in April 2002, they established a common action platform and agreed to bring this issue to the LWF General Assembly in 2003 in Winnipeg, Canada. They felt that the theme of the Assembly, "For the healing of the world," was in line with their concern and commitment to act on this matter.

In Winnipeg the issue of illegitimate debt was given broad attention. In the message from the Assembly it is stated that "the international debt has become an instrument of domination; the rates of interest charged amount to usury; many of the debts are illegitimate (including 'odious' debts); the efforts undertaken by governments and international financial institutions so far have failed..."[1]. The Assembly also voted the adoption of a resolution on trade and development policies/international debt/corporate social responsibility that invited the LWF and its member churches to give priority to the issue of international debt, i.e. to "raise the question which portion is illegitimate/odious debt, support those victims and their lawyers who are filing court cases for reparation in national courts and the International Court of Justice, and challenge the governments to cancel the illegitimate debt both bilateral and multilateral."[2]

As a follow-up to the Assembly decision, the LWF Department for Mission and Development (DMD) initiated a regional program for Latin America and the Caribbean called "Advocacy on Illegitimate Debt." Two member churches in Argentina were asked to take a leading role in implementing the program. As a result, two very knowledgeable pastors on the debt issue were made available from these churches on a full-time basis to carry out this task.

This is not the place for giving a full account of all the important achievements of this program since it was started in 2005. Rather, I would like to make three observations from a DMD perspective regarding its nature and importance.

---

[1] *For the Healing of the World. Official Report of the LWF Tenth Assembly* (Geneva: The Lutheran World Federation, 2004), p.61.

[2] Ibid., pp. 68-69.

The first comment relates to the internal development of this initiative. Initially, it was clearly a "crying out" shaped by indignation. As the churches consciously added their voices to this "crying out" and asked their ecumenical network for solidarity, this cry became a prophetic voice upon which the worldwide Lutheran Communion focused and acted. Later on, when an actual program was established, the initiative took the form of diaconal action, carefully planned, and with clearly identified objectives.

It is important to recognize the different stages in this process: from a phase of indignation, the process developed into responsible participation in complex procedures of investigation and documentation. Without a doubt, it belongs to the nature of diaconal action to enhance the quality and sustainability of what is being done. The nature of this issue requires action that goes beyond rhetoric. It demands advanced knowledge and ability to discern. Only then is one given the credibility to play an active role in a complex process, as is now the case for this program. At the same time, such a level of professional performance does not contradict the basic diaconic vision of resisting evil and of restoring justice. On the contrary, these elements reinforce each other as they clearly underscore the added value of diakonia as church-based action within the public sphere.

The program was certainly motivated by the outcome of the LWF global consultation on "Prophetic Diakonia" in Johannesburg in 2002. The letter from this consultation urges the churches to be "challenged to move toward more prophetic forms of diakonia. Inspired by Jesus and the prophets who confronted those in power and called for changes in unjust structures and practices, we pray that God may empower us to help transform all that leads to human greed, violence, injustice and exclusion."[3]

It is indeed tempting to label the program on illegitimate debt as an example of prophetic diakonia. Its main focus is advocacy and the defense of justice and of the dignity of the poor, very much in line with, and inspired by, the biblical models of prophetic action. The biblical witness reminds us, however, to use this term with caution, because prophetic presence cannot be institutionalized. The challenge to prophetic action is evident, but it has to be left to the judgment of others to decide whether what is being done is experienced as the realization of the prophetic ministry of the church.

The LWF mission document *Mission in Context*, published in 2004, reiterates the concept of prophetic diakonia, reminding that "diakonia is more than mere charity. The church understands diakonia to be interrelated

---

[3] Cf. "Prophetic Diakonia," an Epistle from the LWF Global Consultation on Diakonia at **www.elca.org**

deeply with *kerygma* (proclamation) and *koinonia* (sharing at the table) and thus as inevitably prophetic. It goes beyond initial reaction to immediate needs, tackling the root causes of poverty and debilitating structural and systemic violence."[4] This perspective of placing diaconal action within a holistic understanding of the mission of the church—as proclamation, service or diakonia and advocacy—has affirmed the commitment of the Latin American churches to deal with the question of illegitimate debt.

Secondly, the communion dimension of this program merits attention. As mentioned above, most of the Lutheran churches in Latin America are very small and have a rather limited record of public performance. How could they expect their voice to be heard? Two important strategies were identified. The first was to join forces and involve the whole Lutheran Communion in this endeavor. The second was to establish alliances at a local level with like-minded people, for instance with committed politicians, lawyers, etc. This approach gave weight to the program that never would have been possible if the churches had opted for operating in isolation. It also gave public visibility to capacities that the churches possess and that otherwise might have been ignored.

The third observation concerns the way in which this program was organized. The program became an exciting example of reciprocal empowerment. The Geneva office of the LWF was responsible for the coordination and funding of the program, but implementation took place in the region, with church leaders from Argentina taking the lead. In other words, local partners were empowered to act with authority in the name of the whole communion and, in turn, others were empowered to speak out on this issue in their respective contexts. The experience has led Nordic countries to recognize new roles of action which include the insights and contributions from the Latin American scene.

The present documentation is meant to provide a further sharing of experiences and insight regarding the program on illegitimate debt. Its primary aim is to report back to the wide network of supporters of the program, both within and outside of the Lutheran communion, and to strengthen the network for continued action. But it is also hoped that this material will trigger new initiatives related to the question of illegitimate debt, as more cases in many countries all over the world are surfacing and becoming known to the public. Lastly, there is the hope that these new initiatives could be an expression of the vision formulated by the LWF Winnipeg Assembly—"For the Healing of the World."

---

[4] The Lutheran World Federation, *Mission in Context: Transformation, Reconciliation, Empowerment* (Geneva: LWF, 2004), p. 37.

Illegitimate Foreign Debt as a Field of Action for the Churches

Gloria Rojas

1. Foreign debt as an issue for the church

I have on occasion met with a degree of amazement on the faces of people when I share with them my enthusiasm concerning the work that we are doing on the issue of foreign debt as a communion of member churches of the Lutheran World Federation (LWF) in Latin America. Why are the Lutheran churches taking up this issue? Does foreign debt have to occupy such a prominent place? Should the Lutheran communion be devoting so much effort and so many resources to it? To what extent is campaigning against illegitimate foreign debt part of the mission of the church?

On first sight, the church–debt combination may appear strange or unusual. Apart from some exceptions, particularly in the context of the advocacy campaign "Jubilee 2000" at the turn of the new millennium, the Christian church has generally not considered the issue of debt to be of great importance.

That fact, however, is rather surprising. If we take into account how strongly the theme of debt appears in the prayer that our Lord Jesus Christ taught us, the Lord's Prayer, its absence from the church's preaching and political diakonia could almost be seen as a contradiction. "Forgive us our debts as we forgive our debtors," is a prayer used regularly in each worship service, in many community meetings and in our personal devotions. The issue of foreign debt is there, and thus it is in no way unfamiliar, neither in the language nor in the thinking of the church.

The right question to ask, therefore, is not why the church is involved with the issue of foreign debt. Rather, the right question has to be: how can it be that the issue of debt, so much present in our communal and individual spiritual life, is still so absent from the life and concern of the church in general?

2. The issue of foreign debt as an expression of our pastoral accompaniment

There are definitely also other strong reasons that have led us to con-centrate our attention as a regional communion on the issue of foreign debt, and devote a special ministry to it.

Our joint reflection as churches of the region on our pastoral experi-ence at the community level in our respective Latin American countries has been of particular importance. We see marginalization and exclusion, and how these social phenomena are often growing more acute rather than decreasing. We see how whole sectors in our countries cannot achieve access to their basic rights, or have even lost that access over the past several decades. We share the suffering of families that break up as young people emigrate to other countries in order merely to survive.

It is out of this pastoral work of accompaniment, and our analysis and reflection on it, that the theme of illegitimate foreign debt has impressed itself on us as a fundamentally important issue in order to reverse the suffering and impoverishment that we see around us. The churches of the regional Lutheran communion are engaging with the issue of foreign debt because they can see the havoc that it is wreaking in our congregations and peoples.

3. The issue of foreign debt as an expression of our ethical and moral commitment

The more we have researched and the more we have learned, the angrier many of us have become at the way in which many of the international loans have been negotiated, granted and used. More and more evidence is emerging about a system whose procedures are intrinsically flawed. The abuse of power in the negotiation of terms and repayment of the loans makes a mockery of the basic concept of state sovereignty, whether the nation concerned is rich or poor, creditor or debtor. Evidence is emerging of illegality in many of the contracts entered into. There is an obvious, total lack of transparency and democratic accountability. Groups, and even individuals, benefit from the loans, either through the fraudulent advantages they obtain because of them, or by simply misappropriating the loans for purposes other than those for which they were requested. The fact that the debt renegotiation terms often determine public policy

and prevent states from fulfilling their obligation with regard to satis-
fying the minimal rights of their citizens is another aspect that raises
a whole series of wide-ranging ethical and moral questions. Should an
entire people, should society as a whole repay debts that in many cases
have been negotiated under extortionate conditions? Should an entire
nation repay what those responsible, both creditors and debtors, know
full well has benefitted only a few?

It is in a spirit of gospel-inspired righteous indignation that the LWF
member churches feel that they must raise their voices to condemn this
immorality and the absence of basic ethical criteria in world economic
relationships, both between countries, and between countries and international financial powers.

For the same reason, we have gone one step further, even beyond
what is contained in the Lord's Prayer: not simply to ask for forgiveness, or cancellation, of debts, but also that the criterion of justice be
applied. There can be cancellations of debt, as indeed there have been
in the past, and will probably be in the future. We are not against that.
But we have arrived at the conviction that forgiveness or cancellation of
debts only maintains and perpetuates the illegitimacy and the illegality
connected with many international loans, since debt cancellation does
not rectify the basic injustices and imbalances that today characterize
the mechanisms according to which they function.

4. The issue of illegitimate foreign debt as a further expression of the struggle against impunity

A further factor that has certainly influenced the LWF member churches
in Latin America in their vocation to take up the issue of illegitimate
foreign debt and to deal with it in a consistent manner via a program, has
been the clear commitment on the part of many of them to the struggle
against impunity. At the time of the military dictatorships, the churches
in Latin America became sensitive to the issue of impunity, which, sadly,
is very much present in our societies, but which in that period reached
unprecedented proportions. The struggle against impunity was taken
up so strongly by many of the churches in the region, that today it has
almost become part of our institutional self-consciousness.

The blatant instances of impunity and corruption in the mechanisms
and management of loans at the international level struck a chord in

the churches of the region and compelled them to commit themselves to the issue of illegitimate foreign debt as a part of their commitment to eradicate impunity in our societies.

It is fitting to mention, in this context, that the corruption brought to light in our present investigations does not only involve individuals and structures here in Latin America. It would, in fact, be very convenient to attribute corruption to only one of the parties involved in loan arrangements. There are, of course, serious examples of embezzlement and misappropriation in our own countries. We have, however, discovered that, in order for corruption to be able to function, systems and linkages have to be created which involve players from both sides of the loan process. In order to dismantle these networks, action at global level is required.

5. The issue of illegitimate foreign debt as a contribution to fair and mutually responsible international relations

Our approach in attacking incidences of impunity does not arise out of a desire for revenge nor a wish to harm individuals. Nor is it our intention to undermine the foundations of economic relations between the world's nations.

Our intention is rather to contribute as Lutheran churches—and, we hope, together with the cooperation of our sister churches in other regions—to build relations that are more equitable, more just and more mutually responsible within the global village. It does not make for good relations between the countries of the world that such great differences in the accumulation and use of the planet's resources exist. Nor that world economic relations—shaped as they so powerfully are by neo-liberal ideology—function without any form of regulation and independently of common, internationally accepted legal frameworks and moral standards. It does not make for good relations between peoples when international trade, including the system of international credit, imposes conditions which are arbitrary and excessive. It does not make for peaceful co-existence between the countries of the so-called South and those of the so-called North that the net annual transfer of funds from the South to the North is USD 350 billion[1]. Repayment of debt represents a large part

---

[1] United Nations, "International Financial System and Development," report of the Secretary-General. Sixtieth session of the General Assembly, document A/60/163, 27 July 2005, http://daccessdds.un.org

of such transfers. Will peaceful co-existence be possible if that trend is not reversed? How is it possible that the debt continues to increase in the face of such imbalance in the net transfer of funds?

We believe that, as LWF member churches who today regard ourselves as a global communion of churches, we are extremely well placed to further this common quest for just, equitable and mutually responsible co-existence. This mutual responsibility, which we have begun to assume with increasing strength as a communion of churches and as the body of Christ in the world, is a resource of incalculable worth as we set out on this quest. The Lutheran World Federation, as the expression and instrument of this communion, constitutes an ideal platform for cooperation between the churches, so that together with other players in civil society, governments and intergovernmental organizations, we can be a beacon of hope and justice in our fragmented world.

Illegitimacy in practice: Case 1

A branch of a European car producer in Argentina holding a balance of USD 94 million on its accounts, requested a loan of USD 4 million from a bank in England. The credit was granted, but with the condition that the company keep a balance of at least USD 4.5 million on the accounts of the lending bank (guarantee). Why does a company need a loan of USD 4 million when it has USD 94 million on its accounts? Why didn't it use the USD 4.5 million left as a guarantee in the accounts of the bank, instead of taking a credit for USD 4 million?

Four years after the credit was taken, the company declared its inability to repay the loan. Thus, the guarantee of the Argentinean State came into effect and the private debt was transferred to the public sector. The debt of some became the debt of all. Later audits revealed that the statement of inability to repay the loan was fraudulent.

In other words: the Argentinean State funded and continues to repay today a cash injection given by an English bank to a European transnational company. This is a case of illegitimate debt.

(Information taken from the annexed documentation to the court case "42.170/2004 Olmos Alejandro E. Y Otro c/Gobierno Nacional s/Amparo" filed in "Juzgado en lo Contencioso Administrativo Federal No 3, Buenos Aires, Argentina, 28 de Diciembre 2004." Photocopy.)

Biblical Approaches to the Struggle Against Illegitimate Foreign Debt

Juan Pedro Schaad

1. Introduction

The member churches of the Lutheran World Federation in Latin America have taken up the challenge to fight the scourge of foreign debt. They see this struggle as part of their fundamental mission, which includes love of one's neighbor and consists in combating against the power structures that prevent all God's sons and daughters from living lives of dignity. This campaign against illegitimate foreign debt[1] is thus a concrete example of the church's diakonia, or, more specifically, its political diakonia. As churches of the Reformation, we have important theological parameters that prompt us to raise our voices and unite with those who are working seriously on this issue of illegitimate foreign debt. For example, the concepts of the Reformers on usury have today been incorporated into an internationally acknowledged legal theory known as the Espeche Doctrine.[2]

However, our diaconal action as carried out in our campaign against illegitimate foreign debt is not only shaped by theological values based on our confessional identity, but is also rooted in our worship life, in our prayers and the reading of the Word of God.

In this article, I shall share some biblical insights that have marked in an important way our advocacy work against illegitimate foreign debt. These insights spring from an interpretation of the Bible in which our practical work takes root and is nurtured, and which reveals, in the witness of the Bible, real-life experiences of God's people—men and women of faith—that shed

---

[1] It is illegitimate because of the repeated breaking of the terms of the loan contracts, the excessive interests charged, and the clear fact that most of the contracts are fraudulent, mere dishonest devices that no national or international legal system can uphold.

[2] The Espeche Doctrine provides that the creditor cannot unilaterally increase the rate of interest on loans granted and duly signed. In Argentina, non-observance of this provision led to creditors increasing in a few years the initial rates of interest on various loans from six percent to eight percent, reaching even 24 percent within 10 years.

light on our advocacy work and give it depth and direction. Our interpretation, thus, attempts to identify hermeneutical keys with which to approach
our campaign for immediate cancellation of all illegitimate debt.

2. The loss of freedom and of sovereignty as a characteristic of marginalization

In the Old Testament, justice is an essential element and even a guarantee
that enables people to live together in an atmosphere of shalom. Justice
is a guarantee of freedom, as a value and a way of life that the people of
Israel dreamed of and longed for. Their experience of the escape from
Egypt nourished that belief and hope even in the midst of adversity.

It is interesting to note in this connection how the people of Israel
already in the Bible itself interpreted their times of greatest difficulty. The
narrative in Genesis 47:13ff gives an account of the policy of Joseph, now
occupying an important position after having been sold as a slave to Egypt,
toward his compatriots of Canaan and his own family members, who in
the years of famine made repeated journeys from Canaan to Egypt. Every
one of those journeys brought greater wealth to the already prosperous
Egyptian economy, to the detriment of the impoverished peasant families
of Canaan. In Egypt, they were given foodstuffs, initially in exchange for
money, then in exchange for their cattle and, finally, for their land. They
thus ultimately became slaves of the empire, lost in the masses of the
hipriu[3], the poor, the people with no identity or value, the excluded.

The difference in historical context aside, have not the majority of the
countries of the South also lost their freedom at the hands of an unjust and
illegal indebtedness that is stifling them? Have not adjustment policies resulted in an ever-increasing indebtedness? How many brothers and sisters
throughout the world today are living in conditions that are even worse than
those of the slaves in Egypt, who were the object of God's mercy?

3. When what is "legal" conceals corruption and favors impunity

A reading of the story of Naboth's vineyard in 1 Kings 21 sheds light on
how procedures that are even carried out in strict adherence to what is

---

[3] Recent research on this term makes it possible to interpret it sociologically and not simply ethnically.

"legal" can in practice be highly illegal. In this narrative, King Ahab wishes to gain possession of the property of the peasant Naboth. Since Naboth refuses to sell it to him, Ahab's wife, Jezebel, devises an evil plot for her husband that even involves Naboth's death, so that Ahab can gain possession of the coveted property. Everything that follows in the narrative is in strict accordance with proper procedures and the law. Ahab uses "legal" channels and mechanisms to eliminate Naboth and thus gain possession of what he longed for. The story of Naboth's vineyard is a story of corruption, impunity and complicity between justice and the king. Without such complicity, Ahab would never have achieved his aim.

That story is still relevant today. We have at least been able to confirm this in the debt studies and audits that we have been doing in the course of the advocacy program of the Lutheran World Federation. This narrative can even serve as a paradigm that enables us to analyze behavior and methods that existed then and still exist today.

On the one hand, we can see the pathological need to possess what is other people's property, this insatiable desire to have everything, and, if possible, even a little more. On the other hand, the obscene web of corruption, impunity and complicity among the powerful continues to be used by our contemporary Ahabs, no longer to gain possession of vineyards, but of natural gas, petroleum, communication services, transport, and, finally, even the water of the countries of the South. In order to do this, they use existing legal means and procedures, but corrupting them in their essence, both in the way in which they use them and in the aims they pursue by using them. The business methods of today's Ahabs—which ultimately result in thrusting our countries of the South into foreign debt—are so flawed, show such levels of corruption and impunity, and generate so much destruction and suffering that they are ethically and morally indefensible. Will a new world economic order be able to admit that debt has become a mechanism for permanent, systematic plundering and for depriving the countries of the South of what is theirs?

4. At the mercy of Zacchaeus—perpetuating unjust structures

The story of the tax collector called Zacchaeus in Luke 19 is also illustrative. This biblical narrative deals in essence with the theme of justice, and particularly the theme of economic justice as experienced in the city of Jericho. The narrative gives us a glimpse of how Zacchaeus, through his job as tax collector for the Roman Empire, had amassed a considerable fortune. The narrative also shows that Zacchaeus was clearly aware that his fortune was not only the result of his own efforts, but also the result of a considerable element of injustice. Thus, once he had had his transforming encounter with Jesus, the first thing he said was, "Half of my possessions, Lord, I will give to the poor." As a Jew, Zacchaeus knew that shalom could never be built on injustice, such as that of the Roman taxation system, which, while benefitting him, harmed ordinary Jews, the fisher folk, artisans and peasants, who were suffering under the tax burden.

Because of his job as tax collector, Zacchaeus was socially and religiously despised by all his compatriots. The temple, which was also an object of the inordinate exactions of the Roman taxation system, banned any Jew collecting taxes for Rome from conversing, walking or eating with other Jews. Zacchaeus was the object of the public scorn of his compatriots and fellow-citizens.

That is an important aspect of the story, since it reminds us that any system, however faceless and remote, needs real people, people with names and faces, to function. For the population of Jericho, the taxation policies of the Roman Empire, which were dictated from far-away Rome and determined by deliberations and at meetings of which the common people of Jericho had no knowledge, let alone access to, were implemented by identifiable bureaucrats.

In our advocacy work against illegitimate foreign debt, we have discovered that the system of debt, with its decision-making bodies and anonymous "clubs," which are inaccessible and highly unjust, also functions through bureaucrats who are perfectly identifiable, both in the setting of our own countries throttled by debt, and in the setting of those countries and those centers of economic power (in our own countries as well!) that benefit from the steady flow of repayments. The system of foreign debt has its bureaucrats, who can be tracked down and identified.

The second noticeable feature of the narrative has to do with abuse of authority. Zacchaeus enjoyed complete impunity under the protection provided by the Roman state apparatus. He not only collected the sums that the Romans had negotiated with him, but he was also free to exact as much as he possibly could from his clients. It was with this additional money that he was able to build up his fortune. To take up a point already made, this was a completely "legal" practice in the system set up by the Romans. Zacchaeus, in his position as chief tax collector, did not even have to visit his various clients, since others did that work for him. In our terminology, Zacchaeus was something like the head of an "illegal association" that was totally functional within the Roman system. Knowing that, we can perfectly understand the second proposal that Zacchaeus made to Jesus: "If I have defrauded anyone of anything, I will pay back four times as much."

The Roman tax system, which was unjust and arbitrary, kept in subjection all the peoples whom the Roman Empire had conquered. It was designed in such a way as to ensure a constant flow of capital to the center of the empire from the peoples it had conquered. The payments by the subject nations were to finance the insatiable needs and luxuries of the population in the centers of power.

Once again, the parallels with the issue of foreign debt are immediately obvious. In principle, both are unjust mechanisms to maintain unfair relationships so as to ensure the flow of capital and resources from the periphery to the center. Although the tax burden placed on the Jewish people cannot be defined as debt, it fulfilled exactly the same function as foreign debt does today: to ensure a constant flow of capital and resources from the South to the North. Just as the peasants of Palestine were not able to negotiate conditions with the Romans on an equal footing, so the majority of peasants and producers in the countries of the South cannot negotiate terms with those who are the creditors to whom their country's debt is owed.

5. New wine in old wineskins—as regards the "solutions" usually offered to the problem of foreign debt

The ultimate aim of "eternal" external debt is to keep indebted countries under pressure and control. In this, humankind and its systems of government have not changed much. On the one hand, we see that still today there remains a majority of those who are excluded, poor, suffering, landless, people dying of preventable diseases; and, on the other hand, a small minority, who from time to time drop some crumbs from their tables in order to prolong the agony of the Lazaruses of today so that they do not die at their feet.

Is it possible to patch up the system of debt, correct its atrocities, lighten the burden for indebted countries, soften its harshest mechanisms, and thus restore some legitimacy to the system? The international financial institutions have made attempts through a series of measures in the course of the last 20 years to remedy the all too obvious horrors of the system of international credit. These attempts have focused not so much on the practice of today's Ahabs, who continue to act with the same freedom and impunity, but rather on the indebted countries, where attempts have been made to relieve the intolerable debt burden.

This trend can be seen whenever the so-called G7/G8 countries meet and generously "remit" a small portion of the debt of one or another country. They thus, at most, give today's Lazaruses a chance to breathe, but they are not solving the underlying problems. If they really wanted to find a solution to inequitable relationships, they would listen, for example, to the outcry for a debt audit so as to establish the origin of foreign debt, its composition, and who is responsible for it. However, the political will to engage in an in-depth study of the mechanisms of foreign debt is lacking, for fear that it might be found out that the debt has already been repaid several times over, and that, possibly, in the name of truth and of justice, the debtors should become the creditors!

6. The prophetic commitment to justice

In this context, it is fitting to recall the work of the Old Testament prophets, who did not let themselves be blinded by makeshift solutions, but looked for justice in all its forms. The prophets raised their voices in indignation against the injustice reigning in Israel. While the kings were building temples and palaces, while the court was living in constant sinful extravagance, the peasants and the artisans saw their quality of life deteriorating. With good reason they felt neither protected, nor encouraged, nor stimulated to engage in productive work. It was the prophets who began seriously to question the religious veneer provided by the temple to maintain this unsustainable situation. They dared to point out that most of the rituals were nothing more than a farce to maintain the privileges of the temple and the palace. There were plenty of attempts at religious reforms to improve the situation, but, as today, they remained only good intentions. The results can be described as "a little more of the same." The attempted reforms did not succeed in correcting the imbalances inherent in the systems themselves. The prophetic message is a radical call not to confuse manifestations of injustice with the causes of such injustices. Applied to our campaigning against illegitimate foreign debt, the rich heritage of the prophets, and its further development in Jesus' ministry, are a constant spur to condemn the systemic imbalances in the practice of international credit.

7. Looking to the future—a global advocacy campaign

When God called Abraham, he did it with the aim, among others, of making him the father of a great nation that would be an example to the other nations. Sadly, this intention of God to demonstrate to humankind what relationships between individuals and peoples should be like was not achieved. Neither the Law of Moses nor the unceasing warnings of the prophets had the intended impact.

Perhaps, though, Jesus, in his vision of the kingdom of God, has provided the basis upon which we can test various interventions. His method was to build, heal, rebuild and strengthen relationships among and with the poor, with those who are victims. One of his essential aims was "to empower them."

That can be seen clearly in the story of the feeding of the five thousand (Matt. 14:13-21). "You give them something to eat," said Jesus. It begins with the boy with his five loaves and two fish and ends with 12 baskets full of food. The resources are there. All that is required is for the people in need to believe in the power given them by God. Before each miracle—I prefer to call them the "liberating acts of Jesus"—there are long periods of teaching. The Master is empowering his hearers as he speaks to them about the causes of their misery and suffering, and challenges them to reverse the situation.

Those and other paradigms could become the basic pillars for those churches that today feel challenged to struggle against illegitimate foreign debt, churches in the North and the South, the East and the West. Debt is not only a problem for the countries of the South or poor countries. There is systemic complicity in all cases of indebtedness. Hence the challenge is to engage in this struggle together, so that the world may believe. The gospel's potential and the credibility it can attain as the churches confront this evil are tremendous. Ministry in the form of teaching, training and prophetic condemnation gives us a wide field of action. It is important that the causes and effects of debt should be made known, together with the mechanisms by which they function and their ultimate aims, which are generally not explained. Using this as a starting point and with the help of specialists from different disciplines, we must seek ways to attack the problem at its root and thus create a more just world economic order where there is a place for a life of dignity for all.

A Lutheran Theological Approach to Illegitimate Debt

Walter Altmann

1. Theological convictions and their impact in society

It is well known[1] that Martin Luther's 95 Theses had a huge impact on western European society when they were published in 1517. Indeed, the time of their publication marked the watershed between two historical eras, when the edifice of medieval society gave way forever to a process of transformation that would involve a major reordering of the political, social, economic and religious structures of Europe. Thus, Luther's Theses must be considered a significant feature—a decisive one, even—in a period of historical transformation such as that represented by the transition from the Middle Ages to the modern era.

This transitional character touched every aspect of Luther's age—culture, society, economics and religion. The medieval system was essentially reaching its end point and a new age was dawning. Everything was in a state of crisis. The medieval system had been marked by a high degree of cohesion, maintained over a long period of many centuries. It was structured from above downwards, from God to the world, to society and humanity. The church had positioned itself as the intermediary and interpreter by divine right. The historic transformations unleashed would therefore precipitate a deep crisis in the system as a whole and in every single part of it. Society sought hungrily after new values and a new order and, indeed, experienced them in practice. And at the point where old and new met, we find Luther.

Luther's (re)discovery of the message of justification by grace through faith had a liberating effect, first in personal terms—above all for Luther himself—but also for countless fellow human beings who no longer had to rely on good works or on financial contributions in order to obtain salvation. It had a liberating effect inasmuch as the tutelage

---

[1] In this article, I have drawn on observations contained in my book *Luther and Liberation: A Latin American Perspective*, tr. Mary M. Soldberg (Minneapolis: Fortress Press, 1992).

of the church, which was founded on an understanding of divine law as administered through the church hierarchy, was done away with. Lastly, the message was liberating with regard to social relations by making it possible (indeed, imperative) for the established order—now understood to be based on human law—to be reformed so that it met people's present needs, especially those of the most vulnerable.

Thus, Luther's fundamental theological discovery involved a new way of seeing the world—one that freed once and for all the political, economic and social orders from the tutelage of the church. The secular orders are without any doubt part of the divine order of creation. They are rooted in the will of God and serve God's purpose. But they no longer fall under the jurisdiction of divine law. Thus, the law in the secular sphere was not rooted in some immutable law of God, but rather shaped by the real-life needs which arose as the result of historical processes which genuinely affected people's material and spiritual lives. These were matters for human law and the rules thereof, which, as such, could be reformed or replaced. It was a truly revolutionary idea, and one that did away with the ecclesiastical hegemony of the feudal system. At the same time, once freed from fear for their own salvation, people were free as well to look around themselves and see the world—including the public sphere—as a place where they could exercise their new-found Christian liberty, not now for their own benefit but as a public service to their neighbors. For this reason, although Luther's chief aim was to "rediscover the Gospel," he was not unaware of the capacity for public action entrusted to all baptized believers as partakers in the genuine, universal priesthood of the people of God.

These insights are not irrelevant to the issue that is of interest to us as LWF member Lutheran churches in Latin America—that of illegitimate foreign debt: Luther's theological perspectives, quite beyond their unquestionable theological relevance, revealed their social relevance and transformative potential in the way the reformer himself applied them to the practical circumstances faced by his fellow citizens in his day, especially by those who suffered as a result of poverty and a lack of access to information.

This intersection between theological convictions and their application to the realities and experiences of life provides a first, and highly relevant, theological key for the churches' advocacy program on illegitimate foreign debt. For that work is part of the same tradition of providing a theological and spiritual interpretation for the actions we see being taken in the sphere of global economic relations and for the impacts that these actions have on our Latin American peoples. The significance of this theological and hermeneutical key is even greater when the relationships in question are obviously and directly comparable, even though they are five centuries apart: at present, behavior and rules are imposed from a position of unchallenged, autocratic power on a population that loses all it has in its obligation to fulfill them faithfully. Admittedly, people's concerns and fears have changed. The old terror of the everlasting torments of hell, so graphically depicted by the church in that era, has given way to a modern terror in the form of the pitiless struggle for survival and for a future with dignity. It matters little that the liberation needed then was from church tutelage, while today we are the victims of a globalizing system which, legitimizing itself in secular terms, nevertheless has trappings of absolutism. Then and now, at stake is the life of human beings created in God's image (imago Dei), a life which, according to the theological convictions of the Reformation, and even outside of those convictions, has an inalienable right to exist and is endowed with inherent dignity, all of which is the result of the grace and justice of God.

2. The dialectical tension between divine rule and human rule

In applying a theological perspective to the situations we experience and endure in our daily lives and relationships, there is clearly a risk, for one might consider that doing so would require applying theological categories directly to economic and commercial relations. Luther himself developed a meticulous distinction that he considered essential between the so-called "two realms," the secular and the spiritual.

Again, we must recall the historical context in which Luther developed these ideas. Throughout the Middle Ages, bloody conflict raged in Europe between the spiritual power, represented by the church hierarchy, and the secular power as expressed in the monarchies and the principalities of the day—a conflict in which each power constantly threatened to absorb or conquer the other.

Here, too, Luther's theology represented a major innovation in that it powerfully stressed that both of those powers were needed and had a right to exist—in particular the secular power, which in his day did not possess legitimacy. The effect of this innovation was in practice to demythologize the secular power, laying one of the major foundations that later led to the formation of modern states. It also brought about a liberation from theocratic notions regarding secular government.

However, the strength of Luther's argument for the right to existence of a secular power, whose exercise of authority was not governed by theological precepts or subject to religious hegemony, should not imply that this secular power was to operate in isolation, independent of the spiritual realm. Luther believed that the interactions and relations between the two powers were dialectical in nature and that this dialectical tension shaped the contextual frameworks they needed in which to exercise their respective authority. These were not absolute but interrelated powers, and God revealed God's kingdom in and through both of them, as a demonstration of God's continuing creative activity that sustains God's creation (*creatio continua*).

This fundamental concept in Lutheran theology—the distinction between, but not absolute separation of, the two realms—is in two ways remarkably pertinent to our advocacy campaign on illegitimate foreign debt. On one hand, the distinction between the two realms prevents us from directly applying theological perspectives without any interpretation to the complex problem of illegitimate foreign debt and the issues that underlie it, such as the question of global economic relations and loan mechanisms. On the other, it requires the churches to enter into dialogue and interact with the secular sciences—economics, law (both national and international) and sociology—in order that their call for the preservation of human dignity and justice in international economic relations is heard.

Moreover, the distinction between the realms and the concept of dialectical interaction between them form the basis for the churches' passionate opposition to the claim—so common in our day, especially in neoliberal ideology—that the economy is governed solely by its own rules with no thought for its impact on people or the environment and with complete disregard for ethical and moral considerations. The distinction between the two realms is a powerful theological and hermeneutical tool for developing logical arguments against the paradigm of total economic deregulation. This also applies to the issue of illegitimate foreign debt in particular, for it is clear that, when international loan mechanisms operate in a political, legal and moral vacuum, the consequences for humankind and its coexistence in justice and peace are disastrous.

3. Law and gospel

An "evangelical" approach to the issue of illegitimate foreign debt, however, requires another important dialectical tension defined by Luther, this time between the law and the gospel as the two ways in which God reveals God's self to humanity, whereby the gospel nevertheless always takes precedence over the law as God's will, both initially and ultimately. The law—that is, the condemnation of a human being for failing to live in accordance with God's will—is in Luther's words the "teacher" that leads humanity to the gospel and opens its doors.

In our advocacy campaign on illegitimate foreign debt, great emphasis has been placed on prophetically denouncing the illegitimacy of this indebtedness and the corrupt and illegal manifestations thereof. To this extent its voice has been one of condemnation, challenge and passionate rejection.

Yet this prophetic voice of condemnation and rejection is situated within a broader perspective of the proclamation of grace—the gospel—which the churches must never cease announcing. For in truth, the ultimate aim of our work is not moral condemnation of illegitimate foreign debt, nor is it to bring to justice those who have broken the law in their management of that debt. Rather, condemnation and court action are milestones on the road to the destination for which we long—the achievement of coexistence in this global village on the basis of justice, and of respect for and protection of the rights of all peoples to exist and develop. Without this perspective as its compass and inspiration, our program would lose its way. For it is this that demonstrates the truth that God loves life, desires justice and longs for peace, and calls the whole church and individual Christians, whatever their place or position in the secular world, to take part in that story—his story—which brings these aspirations into reality and, with them, life in fullness for all.

4. Luther and usury

However, there are other parts of Luther's theological thinking that are much more directly relevant to the problem of illegitimate foreign debt and can allow LWF member churches in Latin America today to make their voice heard.

Indeed, Luther on many occasions addressed the practice of usury, even devoting a number of writings to that scourge which so violently tore at social harmony in his day.[2] Luther's economic writings reveal a deep and unmistakable compassion for the poor. His denunciation of economic abuses reveals a strong concern for and commitment to justice.

---

[2] "Short Sermon on Usury" (1519), "Long Sermon on Usury" (1520) and the treatise "On Trading and Usury" (1524).

His economic thought was deeply rooted in concern for the basic needs of people, rather than a desire for profit.

Again, we must take account of the historical context in which these reflections and statements were born if we are properly to understand Luther's concerns and assess how well they may be applied today. For the times we live in are completely different, since in Luther's day the prohibition handed down by the Second Lateran Council of 1139 against the charging of interest on loans was still—at least in theory—in full force. Indeed, that canon law prohibition was in those days even included in secular law, although that legislation was unable to prevent the nascent practices of capitalism from ultimately imposing the practice of charging interest on loans.

Luther's argumentation can in fact be seen to have a two-pronged thrust. First, Luther still challenged the charging of interest per se as an outworking of greed that was incompatible with a life of faith. It would be hard to use this argument in our campaigning today, when charging interest is common practice even in the financial administration of churches.

By contrast, Luther's other argument, which is specifically against usury as such, contains elements that could greatly help Lutheran churches today to argue against illegitimate foreign debt. For Luther's criticism of the practice of usury was based on the consequences and implications of the practice for others. In other words, Luther's main interest in articulating his opposition to the practice of usury stemmed not from abstract thinking about economic theory and its ethical framework, but from the impact of certain economic practices on human beings. What concerned Luther was seeing his neighbors deprived of the means to survive and live with dignity and robbed of their independence and freedom.

This is why Luther clearly advocated political controls on the economy. Relevant here is the demand made implicitly in his arguments, and still an absolute necessity today, for democratically constituted states and international political agreements with legal implications to regulate and monitor the economy in the interests of the population's basic needs. It is in this context that we must also see Luther's proposals and suggestions to the authorities of his day to create community "assistance chests," which would provide for people's basic needs, for instance, in times of unemployment, and in the areas of health and education.

It is with this understanding that LWF member churches in Latin America are making use of Luther's criticism of usury in their program on illegitimate foreign debt. For it demonstrates Luther's deep concern

at seeing his neighbor subjugated or impoverished, both of which processes are realities that we see today as a consequence of foreign debt,
even though we live in a radically different age. Indeed, these are consequences that no longer affect only individuals but also whole sectors
of society and even entire population groups.[3] The voice of the Lutheran
churches in Latin America against illegitimate foreign debt is a voice
motivated by a passion for justice and compassion for our neighbors
who are suffering because of injustice and a lack of attention to their
basic needs.

5. Christian vocation and participation in the public domain

In close connection to his understanding of the secular arena as a legitimate and valid part of life, Luther developed a striking conception
of the Christian's vocation in his theology. In contrast to what had been
the accepted theological interpretation at the time, Luther reinstated the
concept of Christian vocation for all roles, both religious and secular.
No longer was a spiritual vocation the preserve of those who chose to
answer the call to serve as monks and nuns, but it was also for those
who decided to take up a secular office. Moreover, in the Lutheran understanding, even those who did not hold a specific office could also
perform their labor as a vocation. It would be an anachronism to think
that this concept of vocation represented some kind of notion of responsible citizenship in Luther's theology. However, what is certain is that
the idea had a marked influence on the subsequent development of a
concept of citizenship that did entail civil involvement as an expression
of the Christian vocation.

The churches' advocacy campaign on illegitimate foreign debt lies
in this same tradition and is itself understood as part of the church's
participation in the public arena. At the same time, however, it aims to
empower people who also want to respond to their own divine vocation
in the roles in which they work. Indeed, one very positive experience
arising from this program has been how it has managed to bring together
people from vastly different Christian denominations—including law-

---

[3] Furthermore, Luther's critique of usury is consistent with legislation now in force prohibiting
usurious practices. It is well known that some practices in foreign debt are dehumanizing and/or
usurious, particularly in the context of economic structural adjustment policies or debt "relief"
plans such as the so-called Brady Plan (where debt was converted into bonds).

yers, economists, journalists and government ministers—who strive to express the values, visions and hopes that they have learned from their Christian faith as they carry out their work. The program of campaigning against illegitimate foreign debt has strengthened and supported the vocations of many and has focused them on this campaign for justice. In this way, it has also proved a valuable ecumenical experience, which we must maintain and deepen in the future.

Transformation Processes in the Advocacy Work on Illegitimate Debt

Ángel F. Furlan

1. From local to global

From the mid-1990s, some churches of the Lutheran communion in Latin America have been reflecting on and participating individually in activities related to the issue of external debt. Some of them played an active part in the international Jubilee campaign which culminated in the year 2000.

In December 2001, Argentina underwent what was perhaps the greatest economic, financial, social and political crisis in its history. Following a long process which could well be called the "chronicle of a death foretold,"[1] the collapse finally took place. The process had begun with the coup d'état in March 1976. The bloody military dictatorship which then came to power was responsible for the liberalization of the economy and for contracting an illegal, odious and illegitimate debt, which later on would be a serious burden for the government elected democratically in 1983. The process continued with the capitalization of interest at usurious rates, the Brady Plan, successive renegotiations, the contracting of new debt merely to pay off debts, the structural adjustment plans imposed by the IMF, the privatization at an extremely low price of public enterprises and a rise in so-called "country risk," just to mention some of the "developments" connected with the external debt. As a result of the collapse, more than 50 percent of the population found themselves below the poverty line and 25 percent were destitute. Many businesses went bankrupt and unemployment, the loss of savings deposits by savers, social chaos and political instability ensued.

In the midst of this crisis, the local member churches of the Lutheran World Federation (LWF)[2] in Argentina proposed that the subject be discussed at the Conference of Bishops and Presidents of their sister

---

[1] Title of a novel by Gabriel García Márquez.

[2] The United Evangelical Lutheran Church and the Evangelical Church of the River Plate.

churches in Latin America (COP) which was to meet in Santa Cruz, Bolivia, in April 2002. The COP accepted the proposal and included the question of illegitimate debt and its consequences in its pastoral and theological deliberations. Santa Cruz therefore represents a very important development because there the step was made to take the denunciation and demands from the *local churches* to the *regional communion*.

At Santa Cruz, the churches shared their thoughts and experiences and expressed their indignation over the realities of a perverse system which was affecting all of Latin America to the same extent, and then jointly, they issued a strong statement specifically denouncing the external debt of the Third World and of Latin America as illegitimate, unethical and the result of usury, and, because it constituted the tool of a model of domination, they declared it responsible for ruining the lives of millions of human beings and of destroying whole societies and communities.

One year later, at the pre-assembly to prepare for the LWF Tenth Assembly, the churches of the region affirmed that the hermeneutic approach to the LWF Assembly theme[3] was to be neoliberal globalization and its consequences, taking external debt as its main focal point. The churches endorsed the earlier propositions and decided to raise the subject of the debt as a priority issue at the Assembly. As a result of the priority given and of the efforts of the delegates, both men and women, from the region, the plenary of the LWF Tenth Assembly adopted a public statement underscoring the illegitimate nature of the external debt (or of the biggest share of it) and urged that this matter continue to be addressed within the Lutheran communion. In this way, the subject of illegitimate external debt took on a *global dimension* within the Lutheran communion, expressed in the public statement adopted by the plenary of the LWF Assembly.

Following the strong impetus given by the Assembly, the COP, at its next meeting in April 2004, decided that the subject of the illegal and illegitimate external debt was so relevant that a program was required whose specific task would be to monitor and audit the debt, and to develop and implement an active advocacy campaign.

Meanwhile, within churches both in Latin America and in other regions of the communion—the northern hemisphere especially—there remained questions which demanded further reflection. One of the main internal issues was resistance to the idea on ethical grounds: "the Bible says that debts must be paid." This reasoning, which is still held in cer-

---

[3] "For the Healing of the World."

tain circles, is based on a misleading assumption concerning the notion of "debt." The misleadingness stems from the fact of not perceiving or comprehending the fraudulent, immoral and illegitimate nature per se of the majority of the debts of Third World countries and of the system of debt creation. It was necessary to counter this misleading assumption with another moral principle, the one which now governs the program: "debts are to be repaid, but not debt created by frauds or swindles."

2. From prophetic denunciation to political advocacy

At the same time, the horizon was widening. The decision to initiate a regional program which would not only investigate and denounce, but "would implement active advocacy policies," shows that church leaders wanted to do more. Until that time, they had been raising their prophetic voice. Now they were announcing their intention to enter into the arena of political advocacy.

This did not mean abandoning one phase to start another. Advocacy activities were to go hand in hand with the continuation of the task of visibility raising, awareness creation and education within the churches as well as in civil society. As the horizon broadened, the challenges also became more numerous.

These have not been, nor are they now, minor challenges. In the countries of Latin America, the political will to audit and repudiate the illegitimate debts has been lacking, and, with the exception of Ecuador, is still lacking at present. It was in this context that as churches we took up the challenge of launching an advocacy campaign in the form of an "advocacy program"[4] of churches. Although we would focus on the case of Argentina, the investigation was to serve as a paradigm for the rest of the region, and thus the work would be carried out within the Latin American context, while having in mind its extrapolation in some way to other regions of the communion.

In order to meet these challenges, it was indispensable to associate and combine our efforts with those of the ecumenical movement as well as organizations of civil society and the many individuals who were working on this issue. It was also necessary to ensure the message was clear and to put together a concrete proposal; and to develop a strategy, including both the southern and the northern hemispheres in the strategy development process.

---

[4] The name originally given to the program was "Programa de Incidencia sobre Deuda Externa Ilegítima y su Focalización en el Caso Argentino" [Advocacy on Illegitimate External Debt Program, Focusing on the Case of Argentina].

On the basis of the program which had been recently launched, a move was immediately made to link it with other political and social sectors. The "Advocacy on Illegitimate External Debt Program of the Lutheran World Federation," as they began to call it, very quickly became an important player with regard to the planning and implementation of advocacy activities.

3. The need for precise language, proposals and strategies

In September 2005 the COP, with the support of the Latin American Council of Churches (CLAI), convened an international consultation to define a common strategy regarding the issue of illegitimate external debt. The consultation, held in Buenos Aires, brought together international ecumenical partners under the theme "Illegitimate external debt: from prophetic denunciation to political and legal advocacy."

The outcome of this consultation was crucial for the development of the advocacy program. First, a significant consensus was reached among agencies, organizations and networks of the southern and the northern hemisphere concerning the necessity "*of joining the call of all those who demand the immediate cancellation of all illegitimate debt.*" There was also agreement on the need to promote this objective in four areas: awareness building, mobilization, public advocacy and judicialization.

The first two areas are inner- and outer-directed, i.e. they concern both the churches and civil society in general. The other two bring the issue into the political and legal arena. The framework set up by the COP in 2004 began, in September 2005, to take programmatic shape in a wider ecumenical context. The consultation also proposed a series of activities specifically aimed in this direction.

The conclusions of this consultation, in which the current president of Ecuador Dr Rafael Correa Delgado took part, were shared with the various organizations, networks and individuals from civil society with whom the program had already begun to interact.

4. The importance of expanding and interconnecting

The September 2005 consultation helped to strengthen our involvement and cooperation with the various sectors of civil society with whom we were forging relationships. Ties became closer and we began to work together in a steadily more concerted fashion. One example of this was the suit [*recurso de amparo*] filed before a federal court in December 2005 against the early debt repayment to the International Monetary Fund (IMF) by the government of Argentina. This action brought together more than 50 leading personalities and representatives of networks and movements, including the Nobel Peace Prize winner Adolfo Perez Esquivel, the association "Mothers of the Plaza de Mayo," parliamentarians, trade union leaders, anti-debt organizations and campaigns, human rights organizations, movements of rural populations and of indigenous peoples, religious leaders, etc.

This action led to others, both at the political advocacy level and that of the judicialization of the debt: formal petitions to the executive to suspend the repayment of illegitimate debt, draft legislation to declare the debts contracted under the dictatorship to be null, criminal complaint against the IMF for its co-responsibility in the crimes against humanity committed by the military dictatorship, letters to deputies and senators, setting up a tent in front of the National Congress demanding that the issue of the debt be addressed, formal legal action for frauds leading to creation of the debt and to the subsequent privatization of what used to be the national petroleum company (YPF), participation in the campaign to collect one million signatures for the nationalization of the natural resources lost as a result of the debt, and many other issues.

The program also sought the involvement of trade unions, grass roots organizations, autonomous public bodies, universities, etc. Workshops, training seminars, courses and lectures were organized. The program's cooperation with the National Institute to Combat Discrimination, Xenophobia and Racism (INADI) in organizing the Forum against Discrimination on the Basis of Poverty demonstrated that it was possible to conduct advocacy activities even through a government agency.

5. New perspectives in the regional context— the public debt audit in Ecuador

Dr Rafael Correa's election as president of Ecuador marked the beginning a new era in the development of specific advocacy activities. For the first time in almost one hundred years, a government accepted the historical responsibility of decreeing a public debt audit. Unlike the remaining Latin American governments, the Correa government has demonstrated the political will to tackle the subject of illegitimate debt. At a meeting which took place in Quito, the representatives of more than a dozen different networks and international organizations met with the minister of the economy Ricardo Patiño (who later moved to a different ministerial post); he informed us of the government's decision to appoint an audit commission which would include persons from organizations like ours. As a program of the LWF and with the close cooperation of the CLAI, we offered to collaborate so that Prof. Alejandro Olmos Gaona, one of the most distinguished investigators of the debt in Argentina and a program collaborator, could participate. As a result, Prof. Olmos was appointed by presidential decree to be one of the six members of Ecuador's Commission for a Comprehensive Audit of Public Debt (CAIC—Comisión de Auditoría Integral del Crédito Público) who come from international organizations.

6. The added value of mediation

The tasks and activities of advocacy, once under, way had a significant impact thanks to the level of understanding and trust achieved among the various organizations. In this sense, not only did the program make progress in establishing links, coalitions and alliances; it also served to foster relationships. In many respects it has helped to bring positions closer together and facilitated contacts and understanding between organizations and individuals who, although they may differ on certain insights and approaches, nevertheless agree on one essential thing: the fight against illegitimate debt. The churches, who have no ambitions of political success or of taking over the leading role, are recognized as places of encounter and mediation in which strategies can be elaborated jointly.

7. Legal aspects of the debt and the field of international law

One important realization related to the work completed over the years has been of the need to continue examining the legal aspects of the debt. This was also recognized at the consultation in September 2005 which defined judicial action as one of the four focuses and this necessarily included the legal aspects.

This activity is an indispensable tool for evaluating the feasibility of launching legal action at both the local and the international levels. Indeed, ethical considerations or declarations of debt repudiation or non-payment are not enough. Legal instruments providing a solid basis for dealing with the debt issue in a fair and impartial manner are required.

Eminent lawyers have been working on this question for years. Among them, Ambassador Espeche Gil, currently one of the program's closest collaborators, has been working on it since the early 1980s. His work, known as the "Espeche Doctrine," served as a basis for drafting the Rome formula which established the need to seek a consultative opinion from the International Court of Justice in The Hague.

There is also agreement about the necessity to move toward the future, toward a new international financial landscape subject to the rule of law and not the international tyranny of wealth and usury. It is important to point out that, already at the consultation in September 2005, concrete action was proposed along these lines in the form of an international consultation at the highest level and even the possibility of setting up an *ad hoc* tribunal composed of eminent legal experts from both hemispheres.

In cooperation with our colleagues from Norway and with the support on the issue received from the Office for International Relations and Human Rights and the Department for Mission and Development of the LWF, we are organizing an international symposium to be held in Oslo in October 2008. This symposium will bring together eminent professors of law, legal experts and political figures of international renown.

Both the decision announced in October 2006 by the Government of Norway to cancel the debt of five countries on the basis of the creditor's co-responsibility in a failed loan project, and the decision of the Government of Ecuador to audit the external debt of that country are significant events which will undoubtedly serve as background material for the work of the symposium. Both of them open up a series of extremely interesting possibilities in terms of their political implications but also, and especially, their legal implications.

In preparation for this event, under the general coordination of Ambassador Espeche Gil, the program hosted a two-day meeting to analyze the legal aspects of the debt, which was attended by eminent professors and legal experts at national level.

8. The necessity of theological dialogue

Looking back over the road travelled, everything started with the churches taking up a challenge and then:

- going from the local to the regional and on to the global arena;

- sharing their vision, passion and commitment with their fellow churches at the Tenth Assembly of the LWF;

- giving birth to a program;

- moving from the sphere of prophetic denunciation to that of political and legal advocacy;

- developing strategies;

- assessing, directing, reflecting;

- forging partnerships.

This journey has been and continues to be one undertaken by churches and not merely by a program.

The Advocacy on Illegitimate Debt Program has received and still receives its strength, impetus and special focus from the serious, profound biblical, theological and ethical reflection which is characteristic of the Latin American Lutheran churches. The approach of the program is one of faith, and although it may differ from that of others, it is still capable of relating to them and of contributing to their enrichment, in the same way as, secure in its own identity, it is enriched by the individual insights of other brothers and sisters all over the world.

Civil Society Action on Illegitimate Debt

Jürgen Kaiser

1. Who?

"Civil society" in principle refers, on one hand, to private enterprise—credit relationships with borrowers in developing countries are of immense importance for businesses operating at the international level—and, on the other, to the legal community that deals with the legal aspects of legitimate or illegitimate debts.

The following short overview looks away from these two important (and a number of other, less important) groups and focuses on the work of a community of non-governmental organizations (NGOs) and churches around the world who see the issue primarily in terms of a political challenge to obtain effective debt relief for developing countries.

The history of this movement has involved two major approaches in terms of content (as well as other relevant distinguishing aspects), which these groups and organizations have used when addressing the cumbersome issue of the financial relationships between states and their international creditors and, as a corollary, the question of the legitimacy of creditors' claims:

- Solidarity between countries—in the first decade of the modern debt crisis, the 1980s, this was one of the most widespread forms of involvement in favor of justice in global relations. The most prominent examples of this approach are the solidarity with the liberation struggles in Central America and the fight against apartheid in South Africa and supporters of apartheid in the North.

- Critique of capitalism—alongside action in favor of particular countries, direct action targeting international financial relations (frequently in its abstract form) has also played a role. Soon after the debt crisis first struck, when Mexico defaulted in 1982, debt even came to be a focus of political action stretching beyond national borders.

These two sources have been the main catalysts for what, prior to and after the Jubilee year 2000, became a vast, worldwide debt-relief movement. In most creditor countries, we talk about rather tightly-knit or loosely-knit networks, most of which existed already, but established themselves as Jubilee campaigns in 2000 and continue to function as networks or coalitions now that the most intensive, year 2000-related, phase of campaigning is over.

In debtor countries, most of the networks active today, with the exception of some well-established movements such as the Freedom from Debt Coalition in the Philippines,[1] were set up as a result of the mobilization effort that took place around the year 2000. A notable example of this is the Jubilee campaigns in the Andean countries.[2]

2. Quality versus quantity of debts

The question of legitimacy has always played a part in mobilization with regard to the debt issue. Documents published in the early days of the Jubilee movement almost invariably included mention of the scandalous fact that, even after a change of government, the people of a country had to go on paying for the bullets that had been shot at them. Yet this was not the primary basis for the demands of most debt-relief campaigns, but rather the fact that many countries' debt levels had reached such absurd heights that the sheer amount of money to be paid made economic development impossible for those impoverished nations.

The idea of a "debt-free start for a billion people" was therefore not based primarily on the qualitative, but rather on than the quantitative aspect of the very real mountain of debt. This was above all because the sheer volume of the sums owed offered a far more striking illustration of the debt trap and the dominance of creditors over borrowers—symbolized by the chain—than the perhaps scandalous nature of funding for arms shipments to some dubious character with a presidential function.

It has repeatedly been speculated that this focus on the idea of debt sustainability was due to part of the Jubilee movement's (church-related) membership being more interested in remitting debt out of charity than

---

[1] **www.fdc.ph**

[2] The Jubilee campaigns in Bolivia, Ecuador and Peru make up the nucleus of the LATINDADD network, which now covers nearly the entire continent; see **www.latindadd.org** and the links to individual member campaigns.

in complex questions of law and accountability. Yet, even though the 23 million persons who signed the Jubilee petition may have done so for all kinds of motives, charity was never one of the debt-relief movement's characteristic traits. Its origins in the solidarity movement and in economic critique made it fundamentally clear to those who took to the streets in support of debt relief that the debt crisis needed a structural solution, not a charitable one-off remission.

But what is a structural solution?

At least three different demands have played a role in the history of the Jubilee movement:

- strict limitation of the burden imposed by ongoing debt servicing—at the expense of legitimate creditors, if necessary;

- a demand for a fair debt-relief process which satisfies the standard criteria of legality as defined in national legislations (impartial appraisal and assessment of the debtor's situation, impartial decision-making);

- questioning of the legitimacy of claims, based on either a rather broad or a rather narrow concept of legitimacy.

Until the beginning of the present decade, the latter approach, which is the one that concerns us here, played a lesser role than the others for the reasons already mentioned. In addition, debt-relief campaigners did not have a compelling, common definition of illegitimacy that could prove as powerfully persuasive as the absurdly high debt levels mentioned previously (which were often many times higher than the limits set by the creditors themselves) when used in public communication and mobilization campaigns, and more importantly, when lobbying decision-makers.

Change came gradually as the 2002 International Conference on Financing for Development met in Monterrey, and Canadian lawyers and economists revived the classical "odious debt" doctrine of the 1920s.[3] These criteria, defined by the Russian Alexander Sack, are highly contested in the debt-relief community today, but they gave the movement at that time the feeling of having for the first time a coherent basis

---

[3] Ashfaq Khalfan, Jeff King and Bryan Thomas, Centre for International Sustainable Development Law, *Advancing the Odious Debt Doctrine*, CISDL Working Paper (New York: March 2003), **www.odiousdebts.org**

from which to argue. Sack's comparatively narrow definition of odious debts (see Hanlon's contribution to this volume) provided a yardstick against which individual creditor claims could be measured. And even though fewer controversial loans would be deemed illegitimate by this yardstick than some in the movement might have liked, the important step forward was that it was now at least possible to separate legitimate demands from illegitimate ones in a consistent way.

Because of the debt relief for the poorest countries obtained in 2005 after much struggle—thanks in particular to civil society involvement—some of these countries can no longer base their debt-relief campaigns on over-indebtedness (at least for the time being).[4] As a result, the issue of the quality of the demands being made on developing countries has come to the fore—particularly in connection with the emerging problem of new borrowing and the increased demand from all sides for more responsible lending in the future.[5]

In principle, however, the civil society campaign for debt relief continues to use both lines of attack, namely, the sustainability of debts and their legitimacy, whereby the aforementioned demand for fair procedures in crisis cases constitutes the bridge between these two approaches.

3. Concepts

Civil society movements and organizations address the question of debt legitimacy in two primary ways (with, of course, many variations):

- The so-called "broad" approach situates current claims by the North on the South in the context of a long history of exploitation of the South by the North stretching back to early modern times and, against this backdrop, demands global debt cancellation. One variation of this approach is the demand for cancellation of "envi-

---

[4] For a report on HIPC and MDRI, the debt-relief initiatives achieved by the G7/G8 in favor of the poorest countries, see: *HIPC/MDRI im Herbst 2007: Erfolgsmeldungen und Löcher im Verfahren* ("HIPC/MDRI in autumn 2007: success reports and gaps in the process"); erlassjahr-Fachinfo No. 14; **www.erlassjahr.de** [German only].

[5] At their meeting in Essen in February 2007, the G7 finance ministers asked the G20 to draw up a charter of responsible lending. No such paper was discussed at the G20 meeting in South Africa in the second half of the year, nor does the issue appear on the agenda of the 2008 meeting in Brazil. In the meantime, however, the debt relief movement has presented its proposals in the form of the EURODAD Charter on Responsible Financing. See **www.eurodad.org**

ronmental debts," whereby the North makes up for its destruction of the global ecosystem.

- The "narrower" approach concerns itself only with individual loans and bases its demands for debt cancellation on classical criteria such as those of Alexander Sack, violations of peremptory norms of international law (*ius cogens*) or other, more recently developed concepts, as appropriate in each case.

The broader approach understands the legitimacy debate for what it is—primarily a political rather than a legal issue. The greatest problem with this approach, however, is that it dissociates de facto creditor responsibility and debt cancellation. There is no logical reason why, for instance, a European exporter should waive its right to payment from an African import firm that is able and willing to pay, simply because Europe as a whole has some sort of historical debt toward Africa as a whole. If a regulation of this kind were imposed politically, it would effectively dry up the movement of capital between North and South, which is the doomsday scenario creditors are wont to invoke when the subject of debt cancellation is broached. Indeed, lenders would not offer any more loans if they were at risk of losing their claims for reasons over which they had no influence.[6]

The narrower approach oscillates between the legal and political spheres. It is quite clear that real breakthroughs, such as Norway's decision on debt cancellation, can only be achieved at the political level. At the same time, however, the potential represented by the narrower approach, which focuses on individual loans, is that of tapping into a dynamic and expanding legal process in order to influence political decisions. This approach will not lead to across-the-board debt cancellation, if only for technical and administrative reasons: accountability,

---

[6] Other objections to a global conception of this kind are (a) the danger of impunity for genuinely unlawful actions on the part of creditors if responsibility were dumped wholesale on "the North" and honest lenders treated the same as corrupt or unscrupulous lenders; (b) the vagueness of abstract concepts it uses; besides the so-called individual responsibility of the lender, the definition of what "North" and "South" are remains very nebulous. Thus, claims by southern lenders are also playing an increasing role for many countries, and some multilateral lenders are primarily—though not exclusively—owned by governments in the South, while there is also a whole range of countries, including the former Eastern Bloc and the nations of the Middle East, which cannot be categorized according to the overly simplistic distinction between lenders and borrowers.

complicity and harm caused must be thoroughly evaluated for each individual case and where necessary, sanctioned.

Whoever sets out with an exact concept of illegitimacy, will very quickly find themselves entangled in a complicated legal debate the subtleties of which may not be immediately obvious to the layperson. Yet, just as the campaign against unsustainable debt in the late '90s gained a great deal of credibility by demonstrating the meaninglessness of the definitions of sustainability used by the IMF and the World Bank, the campaign against illegitimate debt must also gain more political clout by engaging in the legal debate—as long as, in so doing, it does not lose sight of the fact that every decision to date in international debt management has been based on political rather than legal criteria. The symbol and embodiment of this political dominance by creditors, which eludes every attempt at regulation, is the Paris Club.[7]

The fact that for renowned experts in international law, Germany's claims related to the sale by the ex-GDR of warships to the dictator Suharto were illegitimate, while civil and commercial lawyers remained unsure, is an important insight for the movement in Germany when deciding, for instance, what line of argument may be used to obtain, based on the Norwegian model, an exemplary remission of illegitimate claims in a G8 country. However, this will never be achieved if the social movements that provide the political impetus for such a process do not concern themselves with the detailed legal aspects. Otherwise, it will be no more than another case of diverging philosophical views of the world.

Lastly, there are differences of opinion within the movement itself with respect to specific legal issues of potentially great significance. Two such issues are the question of how to deal with usurious interest and whether a prohibition on compound interest enshrined in a national constitution can render an international treaty null and void.

For example, even within the Ecuadorean Commission (see also Alejandro Olmos's contribution to this volume) there is disagreement with regard to the definition of usury. In the early 1980s, the international benchmark interest rate rose from four to over 22 percent. This was more easily absorbed by countries whose international loans had been taken at fixed rates, but those (the majority) that had settled for vari-

---

[7] On the function and modus operandi of this creditors' cartel, see: Kaiser, J. *Schuldenmanagement à la Louis XVI: Ein kurzer Gang durch Geschichte und Arbeitsweise des Pariser Club* [Debt management à la Louis XVI: a short stroll through the history and workings of the Paris Club] at **www.erlassjahr.de**

able rates found themselves within a very few years in an inextricable situation. So, are debts resulting from the explosion of interest rates illegitimate? Is a country that banked on rates falling or remaining stable just as responsible for its actions as any speculator would be? And if such debts are illegitimate, does that justify the cancellation of the old debts only, or does it also include new loans taken out to pay off the old ones? What would have been the consequence of such a definition of illegitimacy if the reverse had happened: if interest rates had bottomed out from a relatively high position, would a creditor have had a valid claim for compensation?

Similarly, a number of constitutions and civil laws contain a prohibition on the charging of compound interest. This means that interest accrued may not be capitalized and interest then charged on it in turn. This ancient prohibition is almost entirely irrelevant in modern international (and in fact in national) law. In addition, it would be odd if a borrower could obtain a forced loan—without interest, moreover—simply by not making his/her interest payments to the creditor. If the Paris Club—where the charging of compound interest is standard practice—is to reach a decision on debt rescheduling, the relative importance of such domestic regulations will have to be debated.

4. Getting down to business: from mobilization to debt cancellation

Debt-relief campaigns, including those based on the concept of non-sustainability, had no ready-made alternate plans when they first began to put pressure on creditors. Yet the creditors' absurd insistence on collecting the largest possible sums from the poorest, most heavily indebted countries created a situation in which an NGO demand for greater debt relief was always valid (a demand which, in a sense, was endorsed by the creditors themselves with the decision at the G8 summit at Gleneagles to entirely write off the debt owed by certain countries).

For the legitimacy-based approach, the relationship between theoretical development and the political process is far less straightforward. Even within the two main approaches that were broadly outlined above, there are numerous conceptual nuances—nuances that can have significant quantitative implications in individual cases and may even reverse a legitimacy vs illegitimacy decision. For those civil-society campaigns and alliances which, unlike governments and private creditors, direct their efforts toward having the quality of demands taken into consideration, this has far-reaching consequences: international networks of actors normally form around a "living object," that is to say, in the context of a particular negotiation, which allows civil society to make specific demands on lender and sometimes, borrower governments.

Ecuador's Audit Commission is a perfect example. Ecuador is a country that has traditionally had a strong movement in favor of the cancellation of "environmental debts." The debt-relief movement is a major supporter of the current hegemonic political movement that regards debt cancellation as an important step toward a complete break with the country's—indeed, the entire continent's—past, which has been dominated by economic liberalism. Consequently, there is strong tendency to challenge not only individual outstanding debts, but the whole "system of indebtedness."

However, the role of an audit commission is to establish accountability on the part of individual creditors for loans that have done the country more harm than good. In the case of certain loans, for example, from Germany's Reconstruction Loan Corporation (Kreditanstalt für Wiederaufbau or KfW) or the Spanish export credit insurance provider CESCE, a black-and-white legitimacy vs illegitimacy approach is not always helpful. For instance, some of these loan agreements exist only in the creditor's language; the creditor country is always the place of jurisdiction; all fees are in principle payable by the borrower. Credit agreements of this kind are extremely unfavorable for the borrower country, and more responsible governments would never allow such practices to continue, but they do not render a loan illegitimate and hence legally—or at least morally—uncollectible. To escape this dilemma, lawyers in the USA have developed a concept of "partial illegitimacy," according to which compensation in the form of partial debt cancellation would be possible for debts which do not qualify as patently illegitimate (which would make them uncollectible).

Graduated distinctions of this type, though, are difficult for civil society movements to digest, because such movements derive a large part of their social and political momentum from outrage at gross injustices. Yet, making such distinctions is inescapable if the process is to lead to a genuine agreement on debt cancellation between a borrower government and its creditors. And whenever campaigners close ranks around the illegitimacy of debts, they will find themselves in this kind of dialectical situation.

5. Campaigning around the world

The first major campaign against illegitimate debt was launched by the democratic South African government against the debts owed by the apartheid government before it. This, by any definition, was a textbook case of illegitimate claims—an internationally ostracized, racist dictatorship had been kept alive with loans from Western banks and governments. It is one of the more traumatic experiences of the worldwide debt-relief movement that Nelson Mandela's government allowed international financial institutions to convince it that the country would benefit economically if it paid off the debts of the apartheid era. The economic logic behind that argument is questionable, although it was later determinant when the democratic government expressly relinquished its own illegitimate claims on independent Namibia.

Since that time, both narrow-approach campaigns against individual claims and the broader campaign against "historic" or "environmental" debts have been confronted with even more difficult circumstances. With regard to both "tracks," it became extremely clear that political progress could only be achieved by means of cooperation between movements in creditor and borrower countries. Even Norway's unilateral cancellation of its claims on five countries on grounds of creditor co-responsibility was not merely the fruit of the relentless efforts of the Norwegian Coalition for Debt Cancellation (Slett U-landsgjelda or SLUG). Countless visits, expert opinions and campaigns by partner movements in Ecuador, the Philippines and elsewhere made a decisive contribution to the cancellation, which is the movement's greatest success to date.[8]

As a result, the role of networking and cooperation efforts—over and above the "homework" that each individual NGO and national alliance must do in its own context—has grown steadily. For instance, the red balloons at the G8 demonstrations in Rostock in the summer of 2007, were a German initiative, but the idea for the main slogan was international, as was the work to mobilize people to participate in demonstrations and days of action.

An international coordinating group on illegitimate debt reflecting the full spectrum of the different approaches taken within the movement has been in existence since last summer.[9]

---

[8] K. Abidsness, *Why Norway Took Co-Responsibility: the Case of the Ship Export Campaign*, SLUG, March 2007; **www.slettgjelda.no**

[9] EURODAD, Jubilee USA, CADTM, Jubilee South.

The Parliamentarians' Declaration for Shared Responsibility in Sovereign Lending[10] represents the first time that a nearly global campaigning instrument has been created. The network of parliamentarians formed by the signatories to the Declaration will, it is to be hoped, contribute to building a critical mass in favor of reviewing debts and their claims to legitimacy in more and more countries.

[10] www.debtdeclaration.org

Lenders, not Borrowers, are Responsible for "Illegitimate" Loans

Joseph Hanlon

Bankers lent to the white minority regime in South Africa even after the United Nations declared apartheid a "crime against humanity." Bankers made a loan to the Philippines to build a nuclear power station on an earthquake fault and gave kickbacks to President Ferdinand Marcos. The IMF and World Bank lent to Zaire even after their own advisors said the loans would never be repaid, because President Mobutu backed the West in the Cold War.[1]

These are only a few of the most egregious examples of loans which should never have been made—and *would* never have been made by any prudent banker. Surely banks and international financial institutions which are supposed to be promoting development have some responsibility for foolish, politically motivated or imprudent loans? This was the view taken by United States Treasury Secretary John Snow in 2003 when he said, "Certainly the people of Iraq shouldn't be saddled with those debts incurred through the regime of the dictator who is now gone."[2] Any agency stupid enough to lend to Saddam Hussein should bear the cost, not the people of Iraq who had no say in the borrowing. It is a view which the United States also took 105 years earlier when it occupied Cuba and refused to pay Cuba's debts because they had been "imposed upon the people of Cuba without their consent and by force of arms."[3] In particular, the United States declared that the creditors must have known that their loans were for "the continuous effort to put

---

[1] This article draws on two main sources: Joseph Hanlon, 2006, "Lenders, not borrowers, are responsible for "illegitimate" loans," *Third World Quarterly* Vol.27(2), and Joseph Hanlon, "Defining 'Illegitimate Debt': When Creditors Should be Liable for Improper Loans," in Jochnick, C. & Preston, F. (eds), *Sovereign Debt at the Crossroads* (Oxford: Oxford University Press, 2006).

[2] J. Snow, interviewed on "Your World with Neill Cavuto" on Fox News, 11 April 2003. Available on **www.foxnews.com**

[3] P. Adams, 1991, *Odious Debts: Loose Lending, Corruption, and the Third World's Environmental Legacy*, London: Earthscan, p. 164.

down a people struggling for freedom from the Spanish rule" and must therefore have accepted that the loans were obviously risky.[4]

Traditionally, if a borrower—private or government—could not or would not repay and defaulted on the loan, it was the lender which carried the loss. And the danger of such losses was supposed to discipline lenders. But in the second half of the twentieth century, two contradictory changes took place. First, at the international level, the World Bank and International Monetary Fund (IMF) began to enforce repayments. This created what is known as "moral hazard," with lenders not having to take any care about their loans because repayment was guaranteed. This led to the examples of corrupt and foolish lending already cited, notably in the 1970s and 1980s, which, in turn, led directly to the debt crisis of the 1980s.

However, a second trend in exactly the opposite direction occurred in domestic lending. Consumer protection legislation gave lenders increasing responsibilities to ensure that loans were reasonable and could be repaid. Lenders were even required to take into account that for sophisticated projects the borrower was dependent on the expertise of the contractor. Thus the fiduciary responsibility of lenders increasingly required them to look at the purpose of the loans and assess their viability.

The British Consumer Credit Act 1974 defined an "extortionate credit bargain" as one which required the debtor to make payments which were grossly exorbitant or which otherwise grossly contravened ordinary principles of fair dealing. The Consumer Credit Act 2006 expanded this to the concept of "unfair relationships between creditors and debtors." The courts are allowed to change or void extortionate or unfair credit agreements. An important aspect of these laws is that the burden of proof is on the lender to show that a loan contract is *not* extortionate or unfair. In 2000 the United States government[5] established the concept of "predatory lending" which included fraud, excessive charges, excessive interest rates and, most importantly, "lending without regard to the borrower's ability to repay." By early 2008, 26 states had laws requiring lenders to assess ability to repay and not just the value of a house, car or other asset which could be repossessed.

Hence, the emergence of the concept of "illegitimate loans"—those which were improper and should never have been made in the first place and thus were the liability or responsibility of the lenders, not the borrowers. The first

[4] P. D. O'Connell, *State Succession in Municipal Law and International Law*, (Cambridge, UK: Cambridge University Press, 1967), p. 460.

[5] US Department of Housing and Urban Development, 2000, *Joint Report on Predatory Lending*, Washington DC. **www.hud.gov**

recognition of this concept in the context of sovereign debt transactions came when a federal judge in Argentina ruled in 2000 that debt contracted by the military government of 1976-82 was illegitimate both because it did not benefit the people of the country and because it was contracted without parliamentary approval as required by the constitution.

Probably the first broader international recognition of the concept came when USD 30 billion of Iraqi debt was cancelled in 2004 and USD 18 billion of Nigerian debt was cancelled in 2005. Both countries are oil producers and neither qualifies for debt cancellation under present international systems. But both had waged international campaigns for cancellation, saying the money had been lent to dictators and the loans were therefore illegitimate, and that argument was clearly a factor in the cancellation decision although it was not acknowledged officially.[6] The first move by a government in the direction of such an official acknowledgement came in 2005, when the new governing coalition in Norway accepted the concept of "illegitimate debt" and said that "such debt must be cancelled." The following year, Norway unilaterally cancelled export credit debt for ships which had been used to promote Norwegian shipyards rather than for development purposes. In 2007 the Government of Ecuador set up an audit commission to identify illegitimate debt.

Perhaps the most recent development in this direction was the widespread recognition that much of the US domestic sub-prime lending that caused the crisis of 2007 was predatory and illegitimate, because loans were being made to people who had no hope of repaying.

Can't pay, shouldn't pay and moral hazard

The mid-1990s saw the rise of campaigns, notably Jubilee 2000, calling for the cancellation of the unpayable debt of poor countries. But the end of the Cold War brought the fall of a number of dictators that had been propped up by the West and campaigners increasingly pointed out that many of the loans to these dictators had been corrupt and improper. This issue came to a head at the same time as consumer legislation was imposing restrictions on domestic lenders in many countries. Thus discussion of international lending moved forward in two different ways, in parallel.

---

[6] The Paris Club of bilateral creditors cancelled 80 percent of Iraq's USD 37 billion debt and about 58 percent of Nigeria's USD 31 billion debt. Nigerian debt cancellation reflected an understanding that "the loans were never used for productive purposes and that it would be unfair to ask Nigeria to repay," according to Miles Wickstead, who had been head of the secretariat for the Commission for Africa, speaking at the Open University, Milton Keynes, England on 26 September 2005.

The "can't pay" approach looks at the borrower and the inability of poor countries to repay loans AND meet the health and education needs of their people. Even here there is a division in attitudes. Lenders, notably the international financial institutions (IFIs), argued that countries should only obtain "debt relief" if they could show that they deserved it, by imposing strict structural adjustment programs curbing government spending[7] and sometimes also by holding democratic elections. Campaigners, particularly in the South, say that the Universal Declaration of Human Rights (UDHR) and other instruments of international human rights law override this. Articles 25 and 26 of the UDHR say: "Everyone has the right to a standard of living adequate for the health and well-being of himself and of his family... Everyone has the right to education. Education shall be free, at least in the elementary and fundamental stages." These rights must be satisfied before any repayments are made and lenders have no right to impose conditions on the satisfaction of those rights.

The "shouldn't pay" approach looks more closely at the loans themselves and focuses on the lender, saying that where a lender had failed in its fiduciary responsibility, the loan should not be repaid, independent of the ability of the borrower to repay and independent of whether or not lenders think a country "deserves" debt cancellation. There are two reasons for this approach. The first is moral—the John Snow view that people shouldn't be "saddled" with the debts of a dictator. But the second is to impose some discipline on lenders, to prevent bad lending in the future. There can be only one penalty to a lender, which is that debt does not have to be repaid. "Moral hazard" was created in the 1980s and 1990s when repayment of loans was enforced, which taught lenders that they would not have to suffer any consequences for bad lending. The effect of this is clear. In the 1970s banks made loans to developing countries which they had no real hope of repaying. But the international community enforced repayment and bailed out the banks so that they did not suffer catastrophic losses.

They learned their lesson well and, in the late 1990s and first several years of the twenty-first century, made millions of loans, including so-called "sub-prime" mortgage loans, to individuals who had no hope of repaying them. And in 2008 the banks were again bailed out, reinforcing the lesson that bad lending is acceptable. The numbers are very large.

---

[7] What constitutes "good" economic policies has been very variable. In the 1990s the IMF required cuts in poor country spending on health and education in order to reduce government expenditure, but since 2000 the IMF required increased spending on health and education in order to meet the Millennium Development Goals.

More than one quarter of developing country debt, over USD 735 billion, can be attributed to loans to dictators in just 23 countries during the Cold War. Sub-prime lending to individuals from the late 1990s was much larger than this. To prevent moral hazard, it is important that bad loans are not repaid, in order to discipline lenders.

In part, it is an issue of disciplining lenders during the phase in the capitalist cycle when they are under pressure to lend. The eminent economist Charles Kindleberger wrote a book the title of which, Manias, Panics and Crashes[8], captures his view of economic cycles and international lending. Each cycle starts with a period of real growth involving a rise in profits, often coming from new transport/communications systems such as railways. This growth is linked to a rapid expansion of bank credit. Eventually money growth outstrips possible productive investments and money goes into speculation, and this is often linked to fraud and swindles. This is the period of bubbles, or what Kindleberger calls "manias." This usually involves international lending as banks run out of domestic borrowers and become more desperate to lend and make higher-risk foreign loans. The bubble or mania started with the 1973 oil price increase and continued through the 1980s international debt crisis up to the 2007–08 sub-prime lending crisis. This was a period of excess liquidity in which financial institutions (both private and public) were under huge pressure to lend, leading to some very risky and foolish lending—both domestically and internationally.

It may be a natural part of the economic cycle, but the result is a growing recognition that some debt is illegitimate and that lenders and borrowers have a joint responsibility. In the rest of this paper, we try to define the concept of illegitimate debt.

Defining illegitimacy

We can identify eight factors, any of which can make an international loan illegitimate. They are: oppressive regimes, successors of oppressive regimes, corruption, political context, gross negligence, failed projects, usury and unacceptable conditions.

ODIOUS DEBTS AND OPPRESSIVE REGIMES. This first category follows the US definition in 1898 of debt "imposed upon the people of Cuba without

---

[8] Charles Kindleberger, *Manias, Panics and Crashes*, first edition (London: Basic Books—Macmillan, 1978) and third edition (New York: John Wiley, 1996).

their consent and by force of arms." Alexander Sack in 1927 defined the concept of "odious debt" when "a despotic state incurs a debt not for the needs or in the interests of the state, but to strengthen its despotic regime." This has also come to be known as "dictators' debt." In broad terms, any loan given to an oppressive dictatorship is odious and should be considered as a debt of the regime, not of the country itself.

SUCCESSORS OF OPPRESSIVE REGIMES. When Nelson Mandela walked out of prison in 1990, the international banks presented him with a bill for USD 21 billion—money which had been lent to the white apartheid government to suppress the black majority and which the majority-ruled government was now expected to pay. Clearly illegitimate and odious, this "apartheid debt" was paid only under duress,[9] and there are now various court actions in the United States to recover those payments.

CORRUPTION. Hundreds of millions of dollars in loans never reached the borrowing country, but were siphoned off by corrupt leaders and put directly in foreign bank accounts, with the knowledge and connivance of the lender. Nigeria's debt cancellation partly reflected the unacceptability of this practice. Commissions and kickbacks are similarly unacceptable.

POLITICAL CONTEXT. During the Cold War, many loans were made to dictators who backed the West, such as Mobutu in Zaire and Suharto in Indonesia, without worrying if projects were suitable or loans would be repaid. More recently, such loans have been given to US allies in the so-called wars on terror and drugs.

GROSS NEGLIGENCE. In 1978, an IMF representative in the then Zaire central bank told the IMF that there was no prospect that Zaire would ever repay its loans, yet the IMF continued to lend because the loans were politically motivated. Making a loan knowing it will not be repaid must be considered gross negligence and the liability of the lending institutions, notably the World Bank and IMF, and not of a subsequent democratically-elected government.

FAILED PROJECTS. Many loans are now made by the World Bank for projects it plans and designs; other loans come from export credit agencies to sup-

---

[9] Mandela came under huge pressure to pay, including veiled threats from the international community that he might be overthrown if he refused.

port projects designed in the exporting country. Poor countries do not have the expertise to properly assess such projects and are dependent on the expertise of the vendor. Yet the World Bank has a very poor record in this regard, often exaggerating potential benefits from dams and agricultural projects while underestimating costs, and forcing additional loans to correct design mistakes. In the Philippines a USD 2.3 billion nuclear power station has never been used because it was built on a well-known earthquake fault. Clearly the lender, with access to the best skills in the world, must accept liability for a failure of this type and not poor countries which do not have experienced engineers and regulators.

Usury, or excessive interest rates, has been seen as a problem for more than two millennia and has always been subject to restrictions. A central factor in the 1980s debt crisis was the huge increase in real interest rates. Rates had been negative in the mid 1970s—that is, interest rates were lower than global inflation rates—but real rates were pushed up to 12 percent in the early 1980s and many countries could not afford to pay, often taking out new loans simply to repay the old ones.

Unacceptable conditions. Some international loans carried conditions that required the violation of the constitution or national law. In some cases, countries were forced to nationalize private debt and accept the liability as a condition for new loans. In the 1980s and 1990s governments were able to "reschedule" loans (that is, delay repayments) and borrow from the international financial institutions in order to repay loans to private banks. But these loans were increasingly subject to "structural adjustment" conditions imposed by the World Bank and IMF. These conditions included privatization, cuts in civil service salaries (which in some countries pushed teachers below the poverty line), imposition of medical clinic and school fees (which excluded the poor from these services), ending protection of local industry, etc. Many of these had seriously damaging consequences for local economies, leading to the 1980s and 1990s being seen as lost decades. Conditions reaching far beyond the actual subject and purpose of the loan can render a loan illegitimate.

Fungibility and loan laundering

Two tricks are used to try to put a clean face on illegitimate loans—borrowing for ostensibly legitimate purposes and loan laundering.

Lenders often claim that money borrowed by notorious dictators was for positive purposes, such as roads and schools, and thus the loans were not illegitimate. This view is unacceptable. Money is "fungible," meaning it is interchangeable. Just as you do not know if your particular electricity is generated by coal or wind, money in the government budget is not labeled by source. The apartheid regime in South Africa became skilled at borrowing for power stations, which released dollars which could be used to break the international arms embargo. Any loan to an oppressive regime releases funds which can be used for repression, and thus any loan to a notorious dictatorship is odious and illegitimate.

During the past 30 years, loans have been refinanced and reformulated repeatedly. New loans are taken out to repay old loans, or even just the interest on old loans. Debt "relief" often involves taking out new loans with a longer repayment period and using the money to repay the old loans. The kind of loan can change, as private bank loans are paid off with government guaranteed loans. Sometimes government bonds are issued. Loans are traded on a secondary market and bonds are sold on to other people. Thus, the formal loans taken out by Suharto of Indonesia or Mobutu of Zaire have been paid off and no longer exist, but the debts are still there in the form of bonds or loans taken to pay off the original loans. Just as drug dealers use money laundering, passing their money through a series of ever more complex bank accounts to try to wash away the taint of drugs, so is this "loan laundering" an effort by lenders to try to wash away the taint of illegitimacy.

But it should not be permitted. Governments are using ever tighter anti-money-laundering legislation to seize drug profits. In the case of illegitimate debt, the original illegitimacy passes from loan to loan. In domestic law, even if someone buys stolen goods in good faith, they remain stolen and liability rests with the seller. Sixty years after the end of the Second World War, art looted by the Nazis is being returned to its rightful owners. Thus, anyone who buys bonds from Indonesia or Argentina ought to check to see if they were used to pay off previous illegitimate loans.

So we conclude that all loans to repressive dictators are illegitimate, and loans which are successors to illegitimate loans inherit the illegitimacy.

Conclusion: look to domestic lending for guidance

In the second half of the twentieth century, domestic and international financial practices diverged radically. As consumer borrowing increased, consumer protection legislation increased in strength, giving banks and other lenders increasing responsibility and making them liable for improper lending. On the international stage, exactly the opposite happened. Borrowing also increased dramatically, but as the World Bank and IMF enforced repayment, lender responsibility decreased. In the face of this obvious moral hazard, banks, governments and the international financial institutions threw caution to the winds, making corrupt, political, unnecessary and useless loans.

The problems of international lending need to be understood in the context of domestic lending. If I force you at gunpoint to go to a bank, sign a loan agreement and hand the money over to me, then no bank could enforce that contract against you, and surely could not make your children pay—yet that is exactly what they are doing to the children of Indonesia. Similarly, a loan made which was known to involve bribes, kickbacks, or siphoning off part of the money into private bank accounts would be null and void in domestic law—yet the people of the Philippines continue to pay for a nuclear power station which could never be used. In domestic contract law, the banks would have been seen as failing in their fiduciary duty to have lent for such a misguided project in the first place. And a domestic loan contract would surely be considered void if it imposed unacceptable conditions, such as children not going to school—yet precisely this was a condition of World Bank loans in the 1990s.

International lending in the twenty-first century cannot continue with the moral hazard and corrupt practices of the twentieth century. Only by recognizing the co-responsibility of lender and borrower and catching up to domestic practice can we move forward. But the moral hazard is that if lenders bear no responsibility for past errors, they will continue to assume they are protected from the consequences of future errors. Thus, the only way to advance is to recognize past illegitimate lending and force lenders to accept their responsibility. Only this will create the necessary conditions for future legitimate lending.

Illegitimacy in practice: Case 2

The audit of the external debt of Ecuador has revealed that the terms of some contracts contradict fundamentally the basic notions of law. For instance, the terms of the conversion of external debt into bonds, as defined in the context of the so-called Brady Plan:

> "If one or many of the provisions contained in this Contract are invalid, illegal or not implementable in any respect and any jurisdiction, this invalidity, illegality or non-implementability shall not be declared invalid, illegal or non-implementable. Each party waives the claim based on any possible provision that may question a single or many clauses of the present contract as invalid or illegal in any respect."

In other words: the Ecuadorian State had to waive its right to defend itself. The Ecuadorian State subjected its sovereignty to a commercial contract. Something that would be absolutely impossible in contracts between people, and that would normally not even be legal within most countries, is possible in loan contracts at an international level. This is a case of illegitimacy resulting from abuse of power.

Why Norway Took Creditor Responsibility— the Case of the Ship Export Campaign

Kjetil G. Abildsnes

Introduction

On 2 October 2006, at a press conference in Oslo, Norway's Minister of International Development Erik Solheim announced that Norway would unilaterally and unconditionally cancel debt because of creditor co-responsibility. Why? Because the claims derived from a failed development project—the Ship Export Campaign of the late 1970s.

This is the first time a creditor and an OECD country has admitted responsibility for irresponsible or bad lending and has taken action. The move broke the silent consensus and practice in the Paris Club that all debt is the responsibility of the borrower and that debt cancellation is only granted on the basis of debt sustainability. This represents a crucial and significant step pointing toward creditor responsibility and more equality in the creditor/debtor relationship. It is a decision that should influence how other countries and major lending institutions conduct their lending.

Background

In the mid 1970s there was a crisis in the Norwegian shipbuilding industry. Only about 55 percent of the shipyards had any work after 1977. Around 30,000 jobs were potentially at stake—a number that no politician (with a future) could ignore. The then Labour government had to act. The response was the Ship Export Campaign—a mechanism by which developing countries would get cheap credits in return for buying ships from Norwegian shipyards. It was hoped that this would work as development aid and be both beneficial for the borrowing country and would help the shipyards through the crisis. The campaign was passed by the Norwegian parliament, the Storting, on 9 November 1976.

Over the next four years Norway exported 156 ships and equipment worth 3.7 billion Norwegian kroner (USD 593.8 million)[1] to 21 countries. The countries were: Sierra Leone, Singapore, Lebanon, Gambia, Egypt, Ecuador, Costa Rica, Burma (Myanmar), Sudan, the Dominican Republic, Ghana, Vietnam, Turkey, Venezuela, Senegal, Jamaica, Tanzania, India, Mexico and Peru.[2] These credits contained a grant element of around 25 percent as required by the OECD.

Early on it became clear that the projects were high-risk and that lenders could face payment difficulties. After the oil crisis, the world was in a slump and countries all over Europe were designing mechanisms to support their shipbuilding industries. As a result there was fierce competition over a limited number of projects. A swift and easy way of treating credits and projects, while sticking to due process, was needed. At the same time, the quality controls were lowered. The most important thing was to ensure that Norwegian shipyards had enough to do. Credits were thus given for projects that would otherwise have been regarded as too risky.

Following the high interest and the mounting debt crisis in the early 1980s, the lenders had problems paying back. In addition there was a sharp fall in ship prices—so the boats were no longer worth much as security for the loans.

In 1988–89 the Norwegian parliament made a white paper (Storting-smelding nr. 25 (1988–89)) about the campaign, summing up what was characterized as an unfortunate initiative with very little developmental effect for the countries involved. It was also clear that the formal review in the Norwegian Agency for Development Cooperation (NORAD), the Norwegian Guarantee Institute for Export Credits (GIEK) and the Ministry of Trade and Commerce had been rushed and that the views of NORAD and GIEK had been set aside by the ministry. A vote of no-confidence against the Minister of Trade Halvard Bakke was voiced in 1989 and nearly passed in the parliament.

The loans remained and were converted into bilateral debt and treated under Paris Club rules. In 1998, it was decided that all heavily indebted

---

[1] Amounts in Norwegian kroner have been converted into US dollars using the 1 Jan 2007 exchange rate.

[2] According to the white paper, there are 21 countries, but only these 20 are listed. *Bistand-saktuelt* 2/98 includes Democratic Republic of Congo, Guinea and Côte d'Ivoire, bringing the number up to 23.

poor countries (HIPCs) would have their debts to Norway written off after going through the program.

In 1998, the campaign had cost Norway USD 530 million in guarantees with about USD 481.5 million having been repaid, in addition to the USD 193 million given as aid in interest support. The total debt from the campaign in 1998 was still USD 593.8 million. Before the cancellation in 2006, the debt was USD 465.4 million.

Norway's responsibility

In order to understand why Norway, contrary to normal practice, assumed responsibility as a creditor for these loans, we have to look more closely at how the loans were given.

According to its rules, GIEK is required to make a judgment on risk and the soundness of the projects. NORAD is required to assess the developmental benefit of a given project because of the grant element.

GIEK's board felt early on that they had little say in the evaluation of the many projects. Due to time constraints, several new bodies for decision-making were set up. All of them were led or managed by the Ministry of Trade and Commerce—one body to identify projects and handle preliminary negotiations, another for giving advice to this body and a third for making decisions and initiating proper negotiations and signing contracts (the final one was called the "Ship Export Commission"). The contracts contained a clause stating that they were dependent on approval by "competent authorities," i.e. NORAD for development purposes and GIEK for risk assessment. Only then would the boards of NORAD and GIEK have their say on the projects. While both NORAD and GIEK were present in the Ship Export Commission, this was felt to be inadequate both their boards.

For NORAD, the rules changed quickly. On 4 June 1977 the parliament made it possible to export ships without NORAD approval. The reason given was the special needs of the shipbuilding industry at the time. NORAD would still be asked—but it was clear that the decision was made by the Ministry of Trade and Commerce. It was also stressed that this would only apply to exporting ships as aid. However, even before then, the NORAD director was unable to recommend the guarantees during the GIEK board review at which he was required to be present. Of the 68 (36 projects) guarantees given throughout the campaign, NORAD approved only 22 (13 projects). In many of these projects, approval was only given contingent on changes in the projects. These changes were often not implemented.

Within GIEK, the board tried to clarify early on who was to be responsible for the credits given. They felt that decisions had already been made prior to approval of the guarantees by GIEK. The contracts had been signed and the deals had been made—sometimes at a political level. The only thing missing was a stamp by GIEK and final approval by the Ministry of Trade and Commerce, as this was required by the statutes of GIEK given the size of the loans. After October 1977, GIEK frequently included a clause in its loan approvals stating that the guarantee would not have been given if an ordinary risk assessment (as required by the original arrangements) had been used. The board then asked the Ministry of Trade and Commerce who was responsible for approving the projects. This led to a written legal consideration by the government attorney. This document states that even if the process was muddled it was the ministry who was responsible. It also stated that GIEK could not be said to have approved the projects, based on the wording in the documents. Board members from GIEK at the time made it clear that it was "unthinkable" that GIEK as a government agency would not approve deals already made at a political level.

It is therefore evident that neither NORAD nor GIEK approved all loans. Thus, Norway broke or set aside its own rules motivated by the needs of the shipbuilding industry. The result was reckless lending.

The numbers are telling. Of the 156 ships divided among 36 projects in 21 countries only three projects were concluded in 1987. In the same period, about USD 231.2 million was paid in guarantees and only USD 29.5 million repaid or reclaimed. In 1987, 12 countries had made moratorium deals. These deals consisted of 72 percent of the total debt incurred by the Ship Export Campaign. In the end, only two countries, Turkey and India, paid as expected.

The loans also became exceptionally expensive. In the 1980s Norway was one of the most expensive creditors with an interest rate between 12–13 percent. This was about 4–5 percent above the London Interbank Offered Rate (LIBOR) at the time.

The conclusion of the white paper from 1988–1989 was that the campaign had been "an effective tool to alleviate an acute crisis in the shipbuilding industry that was affecting many workplaces throughout the country." The report, however, concludes that "in retrospect the Ship Export Campaign in the way it was conducted had limited importance as development aid."

Campaigning and political results

The decision to cancel the debt from 2 October 2006 points back to this white paper, because it is the only public document that acknowledges Norway's responsibility. However, in the meantime there have been many other decisions and statements that have strengthened the case of Norway's assuming responsibility for the debt. Most of them have been brought about by popular campaigning by civil society in Norway, including the Norwegian Coalition for Debt Cancellation (Slett U-landsgjelda or SLUG). Since the white paper was published, the campaign's claims have been perceived by many as inherently wrong. To a nation that prides itself with not only meeting but exceeding the 0.7 percent target on aid, it does not seem right to receive money through debt payments from the same countries. This holds particularly true when the origin of the debt is taken into account. SLUG was started on precisely this basis in 1994. The demand was clear: all claims from the Ship Export Campaign had to be cancelled without burdening the aid budget. A petition was launched.

In 1998, the then minister of development Hilde Frafjord Johnson labeled the Ship Export Campaign "a stain of shame on Norway's aid policy." This was followed by Norway's first debt relief plan. Norway would cancel 100 percent of all HIPC country completion point debt in the plan. Politicians at the time were very happy that they by doing so were able to cancel debt from the Ship Export Campaign. Most thought that the problem had been sorted out. However, the plan does not mention the campaign and does not include indebted middle-income countries. The focus was on the poorest countries, on ability to pay and not justice, even with the campaign lurking in the background.

In 2001, SLUG started to work on the concept of illegitimate debt. The following year, it arranged a public hearing on debt where the Ship Export Campaign was discussed. The hearing was led by the head of Norway's supreme court Trond Dolva, with a jury consisting of academics, politicians and religious leaders. One of the questions put to the jury was, "Is the debt contracted through the Ship Export Campaign legitimate?" While the jury did not conclude that it was, they found it "particularly upsetting" that Norway was still claiming payment from the campaign and concluded that the "debt should be cancelled immediately and without conditions." They further demanded that Norway should be "a driving force" for examining the term illegitimate debt and that it should be considered by the International Court of Justice (ICJ) at The

Hague. The jury encouraged "radical change in the Norwegian policy regarding third world debt."

In 2003, the Norwegian NGO Changemaker launched the dictator debt campaign. The then minister of international development Hilde Frafjord Johnson was challenged to deal with illegitimate debt. The campaign asked the simple question, "How can you lend money to a dictator and then expect the people to pay it back?" The examples used were South Africa, Zaire, the Philippines and Iraq. The World Bank and the IMF were portrayed as the enforcers and collectors of that debt through their role as gatekeepers to development finance. This led to major opposition parties recognizing the concept of illegitimate debt and starting to challenge the government to act. The response from Ms Johnson at the time was that all debt cancellation had to be financed and that the poorest countries had to be given first priority. She also stated that civil society organizations (CSOs) advocating this in Norway were in danger of not being heard, i.e. that they ran the risk of becoming irrelevant. One of the officials in her ministry colorfully described working on illegitimate debt as "shouting in the woods with a high risk of getting one's mouth filled with cones." The opposition parties however, were still listening and soon there was a majority in the parliament demanding that the government look into the issue.

At a Press Conference in May 2004, Ms Johnson launched a new expanded version of Norwegian debt plan and allowed for multilateral debt swaps for middle-income countries. The new plan discusses illegitimate debt at length and supports initiating a study from relevant multilateral institutions on illegitimate debt. The plan does not mention Norway's own dubious claims. The majority in the parliament wanted the government to go further. This was made clear by the Foreign Affairs Committee in parliament when commenting a white paper (Stortingsmelding nr. 35) the same year. The committee requested more action from the government and stated that (my translation):

> [...] the term illegitimate debt precisely points to the two-sided nature of debt where both parties have rights and duties. A rights-based development policy must therefore be willing to question lending practice and the creditors' responsibility for their own actions.

The committee stressed the need for an international court to judge debt illegitimacy and requested the government to work actively on this issue.

In 2005, most of the parties constituting the above majority came into power (except the right-wing Progress Party). The declaration of the new coalition government—the Soria Moria declaration—marks the real change in attitude toward illegitimate debt. This declaration states that:

> Norway must adopt an even more offensive position in the international work to reduce the debt burden of poor countries. The UN must establish criteria for what can be characterized as illegitimate debt, and such debt must be cancelled.
>
> Norway will:
> - lead the way in the work to ensure the debt cancellation of the poorest countries' outstanding debt in line with the international debt relief initiative. The costs of debt cancellation must not result in a reduction of Norwegian aid (cf. the adopted debt repayment plan). No requirements must be made for privatization as a condition for the cancellation of debt. The government will support the work to set up an international debt settlement court that will hear matters concerning illegitimate debt ... .

While the Ship Export Campaign is not mentioned, politicians from the new opposition in the Foreign Affairs Committee in parliament for the first time started to call the debt from the campaign illegitimate and challenged the government to do so as well.

In a press release dated 2 October 2006, the current minister of international development Erik Solheim is quoted as saying with regard to the Ship Export Campaign:

> This campaign represented a development policy failure. As a creditor country Norway has a shared responsibility for the debts that followed. In canceling these claims Norway takes the responsibility for allowing these five countries to terminate their remaining repayments on these debts.

The press release also says:

> In 1988–89 the Brundtland government conducted an evaluation of the Ship Export Campaign, in which the campaign was criticized for inadequate needs analyses and risk assessments. The main conclusion was that this kind of campaign should not be repeated.[3]

---

[3] Press Release No. 118/06, 2 October 2006, **www.eurodad.org**

It is important to note that Norway only cancels debt incurred through the campaign. Unlike the write-off in 1998, this time the cancellation is motivated by justice—not the indebtedness or poverty of a country. That the cancellation is unilateral, unconditional and not financed over the development assistance budget is also important. In fact, Norway simply draws a red line across the debt. The only loss Norway suffers is the estimated revenue losses from future payments, approximately USD 92.6 million between 2006 and 2021.

The fine print

The devil in the details is that only five[4] of the seven countries that still owe Norway from the Ship Export Campaign will have their debts cancelled. Myanmar (Burma) and Sudan are left out because of the regimes currently in power in these countries. The press release also clearly states that these countries will only have their debts cancelled when found "eligible for multilateral debt relief operations." It also reads that the unilateral forgiveness will be "a one-off debt relief policy measure. All future debt forgiveness will be effected through multilaterally co-ordinated debt relief operations." This formulation has clearly helped Norway in the Paris Club—but could also undermine the principle of creditor responsibility laid out in the rest of the press release. After all, the claims on these two countries are no different, and Norway should assume co-responsibility for these debts as well.

This inconsistency was not missed by the Foreign Affairs Committee of the parliament in their comments on the budget. A unanimous committee states (my translation):

> The committee notes that the government underlines that such relief of debt on a unilateral basis is a one-off debt policy measure in 2007, and that all future debt forgiveness (from Norway) will be conducted through multilaterally coordinated operations. The committee thinks the proposal from the government can send an important signal that Norway is leading the way with a positive example by taking responsibility for a failed lending policy in developing countries. The committee notes the government's statement that Myanmar (Burma) and Sudan only will get the Ship Export

---

[4] The five countries are Ecuador, Egypt, Jamaica, Peru and Sierra Leone.

Campaign debt cancelled through multilateral operations when these countries qualify for such operations. The committee urges the government to cancel Myanmar (Burma) and Sudan's debt to Norway incurred as a result of the Ship Export Campaign when these countries establish internationally recognized governments, and that this cancellation take place regardless of what is done through multilateral debt operations.

In practice, this means that it will be very hard for any future Norwegian government not to cancel the claims on Myanmar (Burma) and Sudan when the regimes in these countries change.

In addition, the committee urges the government to take further action on illegitimate debt (my translation):

The committee stresses the importance of starting an international "barn raising" for canceling illegitimate debt. It is deeply unjust that the people in poor countries still have to suffer due to debt incurred by the respective countries during undemocratic, corrupt and development-inhibitive regimes that have no right to make their populations into victims of debt for their own gain.

The committee will also stress the responsibility that falls on those states which willingly have lent to regimes that lacked legitimacy in the population, and are thus accomplices in the debt problems of some states. The committee therefore gives the government its support to intensify international debt operations in various forums.

The committee will especially urge the government to continue the work connected to establishing an international debt court for treating questions of illegitimate debt.

Setting a precedent

Summing up, is Norway setting a precedent that shifts the balance of power between creditor and debtor? To a certain degree, yes. By canceling the debt from the Ship Export Campaign unilaterally the creditor solidarity principle of the Paris Club, in its extreme form, has been broken. It should now be acceptable to unilaterally give an indebted country better terms. At a meeting in the Paris Club, 18 October 2006, several countries felt that Norway had broken the principle. Even so, a majority of the countries supported the view that the principle must not get in the way of unilateral debt cancellation, provided a country thereby does not gain advantages at the expense of other creditor countries. In a press release on 25 October the minister of international development Erik Solheim stated:

> I am very pleased by the support we were shown at this meeting. I am glad that other countries are now interested in discussing the lending country's responsibility when developing countries take up big, heavy loans.

Still, make no mistake—Norway stands alone on the issue for now. Without public pressure and mobilization in other rich countries, the move by Norway will gather dust and become an oddity. For it to become a precedent, more countries have to follow. If that happens, it is possible to set a precedent that points toward more responsible lending in the future and in time, a reckoning with past mistakes.

One problem with the Norwegian debt cancellation is precisely that it was unilateral. These cases have at least two sides, and unilateral cancellation only addresses one side of the problem. In the future, a debt workout mechanism where both sides are at the table needs to be established. Hopefully, by being the first government to recognize creditor responsibility Norway can have started a debate that could lead to the establishment of such mechanisms and procedures.

Sources

"Utviklingslandenes gjeld til Norge," *Bistandsaktuelt* 2/98, pp. 9–11, NORAD, Oslo, Norway [in Norwegian], **www.bistandsaktuelt.no**

Centro de Derechos Económicos y Sociales (CDES), Trans. Leslie Wirpsa, *Upheaval in the Back Yard. Illegitimate debts and Human Rights. The case of Ecuador–Norway* (Quito, Ecuador: CDES, 2002).

Committee on Foreign Affairs: Comments to **www.stortinget.no**

Committee on Foreign Affairs: Comments to the budget for 2007 [in Norwegian], **www.stortinget.no**

Norwegian Ministry of Foreign Affairs (2004), "Debt Relief for Development. A Plan of Action," **http://odin.dep.no**

Norwegian Ministry of Foreign Affairs, Press Releases, "Cancellation of the debts resulting from the Norwegian Ship Export Campaign (1976-80)," **http://odin.dep.no**

"Norway defends unilateral debt cancellation in the Paris Club." **http://odin.dep.no**

"El tribunal popular noruego sobre la deuda del tercer mundo" [Norwegian Hearing on Third World Debt], SLUG, 2003. **www.slettgjelda.no**

St. Meld. nr. 25 (1988–89), "Om Garanti-instituttet for Eksportkreditt's (GIEK's) virksomhet i 1986 og 1987." Ministry of Foreign Affairs, Oslo, Norway [in Norwegian].

Note

This article is a reprint of a report published by the Norwegian Forum for Environment and Development (ForUM) and The Norwegian Jubilee Campaign (SLUG).

Illegitimacy in practice: Case 3

There is already a tradition of debt cancellation to countries because of the illegitimacy of their governments at the moment of contracting the debt. This criterion is particularly applicable to cases where dictators were in power at the moment of contracting the loan. A strong precedence case is the debt cancellation to Germany after the Second World War, which was conceded under the so-called London Agreement. A more recent case is the call of the United States government to cancel the debt of Iraq because of the fact that it was contracted by a dictator.

Another important expression of this criterion is the fact that many of the international financial institutions have the provision in their regulations that loans can only be granted with due parliamentarian approval at the local level. The absence of parliaments in periods of dictatorship, but the existence of loans granted during these periods, is another case of illegitimacy.

The Audit Commission of Ecuador

Alejandro Olmos

Historical background

On 9 July 2007 in an historical demonstration of the exercise of sovereignty in the face of pressure from banks and multilateral institutions, the president of the Republic of Ecuador Dr Rafael Correa created the Comisión de Auditoría Integral del Crédito Público (CAIC—Commission for a Comprehensive Audit of Public Debt), the task of which is to audit all the country's external debts comprising the period 1976–2006.

With this presidential decree, President Correa overstepped the unwritten rule imposed on Latin American governments according to which the matter of their debt was not open to any discussion whatever and the governments' sole option was to pay, refinance or restructure as best suited the interests of their external creditors. The influence exercised by such financial organizations toward achieving these ends was justified by saying that "it is necessary to be "part of the system" which implied exemplary compliance by debtor countries with the requirements imposed upon them, and giving them no other choice but to implement policies of hunger, marginalization and exclusion.

In Ecuador, as in the majority of Latin American countries, the reckless, illegal process of indebtedness began during the second half of the 1970s. In 1982, with the so-called "sucretization" of the debt under the government of Dr Hurtado Larrea, private debtors were granted the possibility of paying their debts in the national currency (sucre) over a period of seven years, which meant that the private debt was transferred to the state. In practical terms, the nationalization of private debt meant that the state of Ecuador pardoned up to 90 percent of private debt and consequently increased its own indebtedness. Similar processes of nationalization of private debt took place in almost all of Latin America.

Owing to the massive growth of the debt resulting from various refinancing schemes and the taking up of new loans, the fate of which was uncertain, Ecuador in 1994 accepted the Brady Plan, imposed by the international banking system and involving the issuing of debt bonds. In order to finance these bonds, however, new issues took place, contributing to increasing the debt even further without offering the slightest solution because, in the majority of the refinancing schemes, interest was capitalized and, in some cases, at usurious rates. Moreover, the sovereign immunity of the state was surrendered; the country was subjected to the laws of the countries in which the creditors were based and, in addition, jurisdiction was transferred to foreign courts, drastically curtailing the state's capacity to defend itself. This loss of sovereignty meant that the economic guidelines for the country were dictated from abroad, where the net exportation of capital over the past 25 years was also to be planned.

One indication of the incongruity of Ecuador's indebtedness is that, from 1976 to 1999, the country received the sum of USD 50,000 million in payment for hydrocarbons, but to this very day it is still impossible to discover where these funds went and no investigation has been conducted to identify the causes of their disappearance. On the other hand, the corruption of the Ecuadorian judicial system—recently denounced by the president—has prevented any progress from being made on investigations into various economic crimes. An extreme example of this was the indictment and arrest of an eminent Ecuadorian economist who, in her position as CEO of the Guarantee of Deposits Agency (Agencia de Garantía de Depósitos), challenged the banks and succeeded in recovering more than USD 163 million for the state.

The creation of the Commission for a Comprehensive Audit of Public Debt (CAIC) was preceded by the work of the Special External Debt Audit Commission (Comisión Especial de Investigación de la Deuda Externa CEIDEX), which was created by decree in 2006 under the presidency of Dr Palacio González. In its final report, presented at the end of that year, the CEIDEX gave a detailed reconstruction of the various stages of indebtedness. On the basis of this investigation, President Correa decided that an exhaustive audit would be the best way of establishing the illegality and illegitimacy of the debt repayment being demanded from the country and would thus constitute a powerful instrument which the government could use to confront its creditors with arguments based on national and international law, which had until now been systematically disregarded in all the transactions carried out.

Aims of the audit

Decree 472, which established the Audit Commission, spelled out the objectives clearly, stating that it had the aim of:

> examining and evaluating the process of contracting and/or renegotiating the public debt, the origin and actual use of the funds and the execution of programs and projects financed by the internal and external debt, in order to determine its legitimacy, legality, transparency, quality, efficacy and efficiency, taking account of its legal and financial aspects and its economic, social, gender-related, regional and ecological impacts and consequences for native peoples and indigenous groups.

With the clear intention of putting an end to external obligations, which are proven to be illegal and illegitimate and which have been conditioning the development of the country for decades, Article 3, paragraph (b) stated the need to:

> audit the agreements, contracts and other forms and means by which the public sector of Ecuador acquired credit from governments, multilateral financial or banking institutions and the private sector, whether domestic or foreign ... and ascertain for each instance:
> 1. The background information, studies, economic, financial, social and technical feasibility ratings and other documents used to support loan applications
> 2. The amounts and the currency of loans as well as subsequent increases and extensions
> 3. The economic, financial and commercial terms that were both agreed to and applied
> 4. The conditionalities
> 5. The actual use made of borrowed resources
> 6. The overall impacts of the project
> 7. The persons who negotiated and/or signed the contractual commitment on behalf of the parties
> 8. Any other circumstances or information considered pertinent.

The presidential decree provides that the commission should be chaired by the economy minister who, however, exercised his prerogative to delegate and appointed the Minister for Policy Coordination, economist Ricardo Patiño, as its chairperson. The vice chairperson is Dr Franklin Canelos, a distinguished Ecuadorian economist affiliated with the Latin American Council of Churches (CLAI). The commission comprises a representative panel of Ecuadorian personalities with vast experience in investigating external debt. The presidential decree also provides for the direct participation in the commission of outstanding international analysts including a representative of the European Network on Debt and Development (EURODAD), of Erlassjahr (Jubilee) in Germany and of the Committee for the Cancellation of the Third World Debt (CADTM) in Belgium. Advisory assistance was also provided by the tax auditor of the Federal Office of Internal Revenue of the Ministry of the Economy of Brazil and the technical adviser of the Commission on Economic and Financial Crimes of the National Congress of Peru. The Lutheran World Federation (LWF) was invited to work with this commission in view of its commitment to the issue expressed in its Advocacy on Illegitimate External Debt program.

How the commission functions

To facilitate the audit process, four sub-commissions were created corresponding to the objectives of the audit:

- multilateral debt
- bilateral debt
- bonds and commercial debt and
- domestic credit

The following sub-commissions were also created:

- legal
- economic
- social and environmental

Once the work of the commission was under way, a series of distinguished international figures were appointed as honorary advisers, thereby strengthening the commission's competence to examine the external debt situation from the legal point of view, an angle from which the problem is not generally analyzed or investigated. This approach makes it possible to determine in what way fundamental aspects of the national law and even of international law, have been violated when the transactions were negotiated with international financial groups and multilateral lending institutions.

The Audit Commission on Public Debt (CAIC) has a one-year term, which may be renewed for the amount of time needed to complete the task.

Methodology

Two weeks after being appointed, the commission began the information-gathering phase of its work at the Audit Office by requesting the release by the Under-secretariat on Public Debt of documents related to all the contracts involving agreements signed by the government with multilateral institutions, foreign banks and companies. The requested documents also included those containing the legal provisions (laws, decrees, administrative resolutions) on the basis of which the various bond issues had been made.

The commission also proceeded to conduct an analysis of all the letters of intent and related documentation which had been exchanged by the Ecuadorian government and the International Monetary Fund (IMF), in order to determine the nature of the structural adjustment plans imposed by that body and the grave consequences of those policies for the economy of the country. In addition, the commission had access to the archives of the Central Bank where the relevant information is kept about the operations conducted with private creditors and multilateral institutions.

Details concerning my investigations

Thanks to the collaboration of the Commission for Civic Control of Corruption (CCCC), an independent body established in 1998 to strengthen the monitoring of the tax administration by Ecuadorian civil society, the legal sub-commission has received all the Ecuadorian legislation upon which its report will be based. However, the sub-commission will also analyze the general legal principles and the special rules of International Public Law that have been violated when the transactions being audited were negotiated, as well as the legal doctrines which have been invoked in various international disputes concerning external debt.

I have personally examined more than 25 contracts concluded with foreign entities and I have been able to confirm the prima facie violation of the national constitution and of a significant proportion of its legal provisions. Similarly to what happened in my own country, Argentina, the financial groups that granted credit were allowed not only to impose their own unilateral conditions, but also even to draft the legal opinions which were to be issued by Ecuadorian public state officials, for example the Office of the Attorney General.

I have listed some of the characteristics of the contracts, the most significant of which are as follows:

- They accepted the applicability of the laws of the United States, the United Kingdom and, in one case, of Spain.

- They agreed to the jurisdiction of foreign tribunals at the discretion of the creditor.

- The creditors drafted the legal opinions of state officials, who simply signed them. This constitutes an act of forgery.

- They agreed on the capitalization of interest, thereby accepting compounded interest, which constitutes an express violation of the constitution of Ecuador and of the fundamental principles of law.

- Some contracts specified that the loan was intended for a particular purpose whereas, in fact, it was used for something else.

- They established that the agreements made by the government were civil and commercial (iure gestionis) in nature and not sovereign (iure imperii) which implies that the country had the same status as the creditor, whereas these are two different entities.

- The sovereign immunity of the state was abandoned, not only in view of possible disputes but also in the loan default proceedings initiated against Ecuador.

- It was agreed that the agent bank would determine the amount of interest and, in each case, inform the state of that amount, often applying rates much higher than those in conventional agreements.

- The membership of Ecuador in the IMF was made compulsory as an indispensable condition for the granting of the loan.

The above list is merely indicative, not exhaustive, because the analysis of other operations may still reveal other aspects of agreements which are challengeable.

Although the agreements had supposedly been discussed between the Ecuadorian government and the foreign lender, reality was substantially different. In the majority of cases, the lenders delivered a complete package and specified what the procedure should be. The local authorities were left with merely validating the dictates of the bank. In other words, autonomy of will was lacking in the contractual process, since the agreements were imposed and had to be respected, with a few legal formalities being observed in order to give some semblance of independent negotiation, whereas, in reality, the demands of the various financial groups participating in the transactions were acceded to.

The IMF also played a distinct role in these activities since the creditors always required the contracts to specify that the country was a member of the IMF and that it would fulfill its obligations to this multilateral body.

One example of how the multilateral organizations handled the granting of credit, supposedly in the form of technical assistance, but which, in reality, led the recipient country into exorbitant debt, was the loan agreement for the irrigation subsector technical assistance project concluded by the government of Ecuador and the International Bank for Reconstruction and Development[1]. The sum granted in the form of a loan was USD 20,000,000 of which USD 12,200,000 was earmarked for consultancy services and studies that is, more than 60 percent of the loan! To this day it is not known whether any of these services were provided, either totally or partially, what they were for, or what relevance they had for the outcome of the assistance promised[2]. In connection with this same credit, there is also a series of items which are difficult to ascertain and are being audited, but the data available at present makes it fair to presume that these are part of the many illegitimate operations conducted.

---

[1] Treaty No. 31640. International Bank for Reconstruction and Development and Ecuador: Loan Agreement—Irrigation Subsector Technical Assistance Project (with schedules and General Conditions Applicable to Loan and Guarantee Agreements dated 1 January 1985). Signed at Washington on 19 October 1994.

[2] The CAIC has requested the Ministry of Agriculture to provide documentary evidence of the work done.

Final considerations

The Audit Commission, although it is attached to the Ministry of the Economy and Finance and is subject to it, enjoys complete autonomy with regard to its working methods and has the right to request all the documentation deemed necessary in order to carry out its mandate.

The task is extremely vast, because the auditing of 30 years of debt with all its consequences, not merely economic, but also social, environmental, ecological and other, implies not only conducting an analysis of the legal aspects of the contracts, but also a detailed follow-up of the destination of the funds and how they were used by the various governments. This follow-up exercise not only applies to the funds borrowed, but also to the successive renegotiations during which nobody knows with certainty what was being paid or what was being refinanced, and which were accepted under extortionate terms ensuring a permanent transfer of wealth to the various banks and corporations involved.

Such an undertaking is never easy because of the many obstacles which are raised, not only on the part of private institutions from whom the necessary information to conduct comparative analyses of the documentation is requested, but also on the part of many former officials who are reluctant to testify about how the negotiations in which they participated had been conducted. Another disturbing circumstance is the disappearance of key documents from the archives. The consequence of this is that, in some cases, it will be difficult to reconstruct the information.

The work of the Commission for a Comprehensive Audit of Public Debt has tremendous potential. Although we have only just begun our work, we can expect the conclusions of the audit to demonstrate with absolute clarity and on a solid basis how a country's sovereignty was subjected to the manipulation and speculation of international financial institutions. It will also demonstrate the role of the multilateral institutions that worked to perfect the mechanisms of indebtedness, heedless of the enormous prejudice caused to Ecuador as a result of their illegitimate operations.

Debt Cancellation and the Malawi Economy

Joseph P. Bvumbwe

Malawi is a landlocked country occupying the southern part of the Great Rift Valley. It borders with Mozambique, Zambia and Tanzania. The country covers a total area of 118,484 square kilometers. Malawi is divided into three administrative regions: North, South and Center. Almost all fertile land is already under cultivation, and continuing population pressure poses a threat of soil erosion and exhaustion. The demand for firewood has significantly depleted the timber stock.

The population of Malawi in 2005 was estimated by the United Nations Development Programme (UNDP) at 13.2 million.[1] It is one of the highest in Africa. The annual population growth rate is 3.2 percent. The population is predominantly rural, with 85 percent living in the countryside. The population pressure on cultivable land is critical and 40 percent of the smallholder farming population has a landholding size of less than 0.5 hectare per household.

The economy of Malawi is heavily dependent on agriculture, with the smallholder sector accounting for almost 43 percent of GDP and 90 percent of the country's exports. Tobacco is the main foreign exchange earner. Maize is the main staple food and is the most common crop in subsistence agriculture.[2] Malawi is one of the poorest countries in the world.

In September 2006, Malawi became eligible for debt cancellation under the Heavily Indebted Poor Countries (HIPC) initiative. It was USD 2.6 billion in debt. Malawi is paying 16 billion Malawi kwacha (MWK) to repay foreign loans. It is not easy to quantify the impact in the field since the poverty indicator index is the same now as it was five years ago. The present government is still servicing debt incurred by the previous government in the amount of MWK 71 billion. It is very difficult to determine whether this debt was legitimate or illegitimate.

Despite debt cancellation Malawi remains the twelfth poorest country in the world. The extent of absolute poverty is shocking, the

---

[1] *Human Development Reports. 2007-2008 Report—Demographic Trends,* **http://hdrstats.undp.org**

[2] Government of Malawi, *The National Land Policy* (Zomba: Government Printers, 2002) pp. 15–17.

gap between rich and poor continues to widen. It is estimated that 6.4 million people are below the poverty line, while 2.7 million (22 percent) live in ultra poverty,[3] that is, such dire poverty that they cannot afford the daily recommended food requirements. Economic liberalization has left Malawians poorer despite debt cancellation. Debt cancellation has not reversed the massive job losses that resulted from privatization. It has hampered economic and social development in Malawi, as the government has cut back heavily on spending on vital social services such as health, education and social protection (welfare). Debt cancellation has deprived Malawi of its freedom of expenditure as an independent country, because the budget is under the scrutiny of the International Monetary Fund (IMF) and the World Bank. This has helped perpetuate a dependency syndrome that leads to neocolonialism.

The Government of Malawi is no longer in control of the country's economic forces. It nonetheless adopted the Fertilizer Subsidy Policy for low-income farmers, in 2005, despite the opposition of the donor community, particularly the IMF, the World Bank and USAID. The outcome was a phenomenal jump in corn production resulting in a food surplus and making Malawi today a very good example for other countries within the South African Development Community (SADC).[4]

In Malawi, it is not easy for the general public to know that illegitimate debt is being contracted within the government, since the terms and the conditions of loans are not always gazetted. Such loans contravene principles of fair dealing. It is very easy for the Government of Malawi to contract illegitimate loans because of the impasse in the parliament, but also because of the vast needs in society. When one is poor, one has no choice but to go for any offer that presents itself. Close ties to some Arabic countries and of late, China, create an even more serious challenge. Since 2004, the opposition has consistently voted against the budget and other important bills because they have a majority and want to frustrate the government's efforts. In this kind of situation, it is very easy to speculate that illegitimate loans are being taken by the government without the approval of the parliament. This will only be known if the present government is voted out in the next general election to be held in 2009. The unstable situation of our government creates a climate conducive to illegitimate debts.

---

[3] Malawi Economic Justice, "Promoting Participatory Governance in Malawi," **www.mejn.mw**

[4] Arindam Banerjee, "From Famines to Food Surplus: The Malawi Experience," **www.networkideas.org** (accessed 3 September 2008).

Malawi legislation requires that legitimate loans from the World Bank, the African Development Bank and the IMF be approved by a properly elected parliament. This ensures judicious scrutiny of the purpose, terms and conditions of loans through greater parliamentary participation in the loan contracting process. It is no secret that current international aid programs, particularly those involving Western donors and lenders including the World Bank and the IMF, have, unwittingly or intentionally, undermined the institutional capacity of Malawi to manage its reforms and growth in terms of development. This practice has led Malawi to introduce window-dressing reforms just to keep aid flowing, but not enough to end the permanent economic crisis. Malawi is seeking help from China, who is a kind of "big brother" for many African countries. China is giving out loans to African countries without imposing conditions. As a result, odious and corrupt regimes are being given loans which should be considered illegitimate. If international donors do not change their policies, Malawi will go back to the situation which existed before debt cancellation and in which it was devoting 35 percent of the budget to domestic and external debt interest payments.

The Malawi economy will not change unless international development aid bodies put an end to a donor and recipient relationship which places Malawi as recipient in a disadvantageous position and undermines its right to chart its own path to development. Donors should stop earmarking their support, because it hampers the government's flexibility in allocating resources to key priority areas and results in under-funding of other critical areas important for economic growth and poverty reduction.

The lack of a structured engagement and of access to information on financial policies has inhibited the ability of key institutions such as the parliament to demand transparency and accountability. The governments thus need to provide a better level of engagement and facilitation of civil society in managing international financial assistance for development, in order that civil society might meaningfully participate in the discussion on the taking on of huge loans from donor countries and institutions.

The biggest threat to human dignity and to young African democracies is the lack of participation in economic decisions, lack of equity in the distribution of scarce resources and lack of protection from social injustices in the societies in which we live. The Tenth Assembly of the Lutheran World Federation, describing the new global market-oriented philosophy, stated that "This false ideology is grounded on the assumption that the market, built on private property, unrestrained competition, and the centrality of contracts, is the absolute law governing human life, society, and the natural environment. This is idolatry, and leads to systematic exclusion of those who own no property, the destruction of cultural diversity, the dismantling of fragile democracies and the destruction of the earth".[5] International justice and solidarity is needed, and this includes thoughtful consideration of the grave situation of the world's poor and the global resolution of the terrible burden of external debt of the Third World countries; and acknowledgement of how globalization has affected human suffering and Christian solidarity.

---

[5] Lutheran World Federation (LWF), *For the Healing of the World* (Geneva: LWF, 2004), p. 61.

Illegitimate Debt in the Philippines

1. Introduction

The people of the Philippines[1] have suffered decades of accumulated foreign debt and unremitting debt servicing. Billions of dollars are paid out every year to Northern creditors, adding up to well over a USD 100 billion already paid out since the 1970s. The scale of the problem is such that there are already two distinct, albeit inter-related, levels: the overall antidevelopmental burden that transcends specific loans, as well as the dubious circumstances, conditions and use of particular debts.

It is already widely recognized by domestic and international social movements that a large part of the country's foreign debt must be considered illegitimate. Overall, the foreign debt has been a yoke on Philippine economic development. Vital economic surpluses have been extracted and the economy kept backward.

But specific loans have in and of themselves also been problematic. The loans going to support the outright dictatorship of the Marcos regime and its avarice are only the most brazen. Many have also been forced on the people by creditors collaborating with Philippine administrations other than the Marcos regime. Loans have also involved patently usurious terms or been made on the basis of fraudulent claims and representations. The worst of them are not only onerous but have been spent on projects blatantly harmful to the people whose social, economic, cultural, civil and political rights have been violated. They have grossly breached the spirit and, many times, the letter of the law and of genuine democratic processes. Yet, they are debts that were and are still being paid.

The illegitimacy of debt derives from the resulting underdevelopment of the Philippines, the disguised authoritarianism of the current government and such dubious enterprises as the iconic fraud-ridden Bataan Nuclear Power Plant (BNPP). The majority of the foreign debt is public debt which directly results in the single largest part of the national government budget perennially going just to debt servicing.

---

[1] Taken from: IBON Foundation, "Illegitimate Debt and Underdevelopment in the Philippines," © 2007 by AFRODAD, reprinted with permission.

These repayments are made at the cost of vital education, health, housing and welfare services as well as at the expense of critical economic and public infrastructure and utilities.

In the end this means that the country is trapped in a situation where it pays billions of US dollars for debt that has largely gone not toward improving the well-being of the people—who directly and indirectly pay for these loans—but rather toward the profits of corrupt regimes, of bureaucrats and of big transnational banks and corporations.

2. Justice denied: the Bataan nuclear power plant (BNPP)

An example of this is provided by the case of the Bataan Nuclear Power Plant (BNPP) which constitutes the single largest foreign debt in the country's history. Despite manifest problems and dubious circumstances recognized up to the level of the Supreme Court, the loan agreement itself has never been subjected to judicial scrutiny and annulled by proper court decree. The loan contract has then been presumed valid and the attendant debt servicing has therefore continued. And yet the BNPP debts were contracted by fraudulent parties, through fraudulent means, with fraudulent terms and for fraudulent purposes.

On 9 February 1976, the Marcos regime, through the National Power Corporation (NPC), entered into a contract with Westinghouse Electric S.A. (WESA), an affiliate or subsidiary of Westinghouse Electric Corporation, to construct a 620-megawatt (MW) nuclear power plant at Morong, Bataan and to supply related equipment, machineries and services.

Westinghouse apparently won the contract through the intervention of Marcos aide Herminio Disini who, the corporation admitted, was paid USD 17.3 million in "commissions" through a variety of channels. It has also been estimated that Marcos himself may have received up to USD 80 million in BNPP-related bribes and kickbacks. In 1974, General Electric's offer to build a 600-MW plant for a total of USD 700 million was outbid by Westinghouse which quoted USD 500 million (this was despite evidence that Westinghouse-built plants in the US were breaking down with alarming regularity in the 1970s). However, the proposal formally presented by Westinghouse in May 1975 was much higher and reached USD 1.2 billion. This amount had already been questioned because, during that same period, Westinghouse had built similar or even larger plants in Spain, South Korea and Taiwan for much less.

Construction of the plant was eventually started in 1977, despite findings by the Philippine Atomic Energy Commission (PAEC) that the construction area was inappropriate for a nuclear plant because it was near a major earthquake fault line and within 150 kilometers of five volcanoes, four of which were considered active including one just nine kilometers away.[2] The site was also in Central Luzon which was a populated area adjacent to the National Capital Region (NCR). When the BNPP was finally completed in 1984 the total cost had apparently run to USD 2.3 billion. Construction and insurance companies associated with Marcos and his cronies were among those able to get contracts. The Aquino administration, however, chose not to operate the completed BNPP because of the serious reservations on its safety (citing the inappropriate site as well as thousands of defects). In 1988, it also filed a civil suit and instituted a complaint against Westinghouse in New Jersey, USA, after which Westinghouse in turn filed an arbitration case in Geneva, Switzerland.

However in an apparent bid to eliminate any impression that the government was inclined to take an adversarial posture vis-à-vis its creditors, the Ramos administration in 1995 chose to enter into a settlement agreement with Westinghouse.[3] The settlement package was worth USD 100 million consisting of USD 40 million in cash, two new turbines worth USD 60 million and relinquishing by Westinghouse of the right to recover some USD 200,000 in lawyer's fees. In exchange, the parties would dismiss the pending lawsuits, appeals and arbitration between the Philippine government and Westinghouse (including its affiliates and Burns and Roe) on the BNPP controversy and that the government would direct NPC and other government agencies to lift a ban that had been made against Westinghouse equipment and technology.

The project's creditors that knowingly financed the overpriced and questionable power plant are the US Export-Import Bank (USD 889 million), American Express (USD 278 million), Bank of Tokyo (USD 269 million), Union Bank of Switzerland (USD 186 million) and Mitsui & Co. (USD 35 million); Citicorp, Sumitomo Corp., and Morgan Guaranty

---

[2] The Philippine Fault and the West Luzon Fault are both earthquake-prone. Mt Natib is the volcano nine kilometers from the project site in Napong Point of Morong town, Bataan province.

[3] On 11 October 1995, the Presidential Committee on the Bataan Nuclear Power Plant (PCBNPP Committee) issued a "Resolution Adopting the Essential Terms and Conditions Arrived at by the Government Panel and Westinghouse Representatives during the Exploratory Discussions from September 29, 1995 to October 9, 1995 for a Compromise Settlement of the BNPP Controversy and Favorably Recommending Approval Thereof to His Excellency, the President."

also provided USD 261 million in commercial loans.[4] The Filipino people paid the BNPP creditors USD 1.9 billion, 23.0 billion yen (JPY) and 107.1 million Swiss francs (CHF) over the period 1986 to 2006. The balance of the accounts was rescheduled under Paris Club agreements and others were converted into Brady Bonds and so are instead being paid under these new terms. Aside from debt servicing, the national government has reportedly been annually paying PHP 50 million, or about USD 1 million at current exchange rates, for the plant's maintenance.

At the end of 2006, the BNPP loans were scheduled to close by 2018 with an outstanding balance of USD 21.2 million and JPY 29.7 million. Of the outstanding balance, the US Eximbank accounted for USD 10.8 million, American Express for USD 2.4 million, Union Bank of Switzerland for USD 1.6 million, Bank of Tokyo for USD 1.0 million and Mitsui & Co. for JPY 29.7 million; Brady Bonds accounted for USD 5.4 million.[5] However, in the first quarter of 2007 the loans due to the five foreign banks were finally closed with an automatic appropriation from the national budget while the Brady Bonds due to be repaid in 2017 and 2018 were also fully paid in advance[6]—hence virtually ending, in the worst possible way, the saga of the odious BNPP debts.

The BNPP project is imbued through and through with fraud, deceit, bribery, overpricing, abuse of power, and violations and circumventions of proper procedures and legal requirements. The Supreme Court itself directed that criminal charges be filed against Herminio Disini in relation to the awarding of the nuclear power plant project. The court found that there was sufficient evidence establishing a probable cause for the filing of charges against Disini, who:

> had capitalized, exploited and taken advantage of his close personal relations with the former President x x x [and had] requested and received pecuniary considerations from Westinghouse and Burns & Roe, which were endeavoring to close the PNPP (sic) contract with the Philippine government.[7]

Among the evidence submitted were affidavits of key witnesses and various documents supporting the charges of corruption, bribery and

---

[4] IBON, "BNPP: Canceling an Odious Debt," IBON Facts & Figures Special Release 28, no. 11 (2005).

[5] Ibid.

[6] Interview of IBON Foundation with Debt Monitoring and Analysis Division – Bureau of the Treasury (DMAD-BTr), 7 May 2007.

[7] 397 SCRA 171, 201, 10 February 2003, per J. Panganiban.

other unlawful acts committed during the negotiation for and execution of the BNPP contract.

A Supreme Court Associate Justice, Reynato Puno, has even already publicly urged the Arroyo administration to stop payments for Marcos loans used to build the BNPP. According to Puno, "[foreign creditors] knew or had no reason not to know that the loans will be used for some illegitimate purpose like supporting notoriously brazen kleptocratic military regimes.... These creditors need not be paid because they are parties to the crime."[8]

Yet while there is already an order for prosecution and general acknowledgement of the illegitimacy of the BNPP debt, there has not yet been any real progress on this matter. Much less has there been progress on the complex and tedious step of subsequently declaring the loan contract void and cancelling the unjust debt. To date it appears that there remains no legal precedent on whether the validity of the loan contracts with foreign creditors to finance the construction of the BNPP is subject to judicial review. After this should be the even more uncharted territory of refunding the complete interest and principal payments that have already been made.

3. The illegitimacy of Philippine debts

The irreducible core that defines the "illegitimacy" of Philippine external debts is that they are, as a whole, an unjust and antidevelopmental burden on the Filipino people. This is not the same thing as saying that all debts are by their intrinsic nature an intolerable burden and that, absolutely and in all instances, are to be condemned. Rather, it is to recognize that in the current concrete conditions of Philippine underdevelopment, where foreign and domestic elites monopolize and wield economic and political power for their benefit at the expense of the people, debt is one of their most efficient and effective instruments for exploitation. The right of the Filipino people to break free from their debilitating debt burden fundamentally derives from how this debt operates to grossly and systematically deny them their most basic economic, social and cultural

---

[8] In a speech during the 10th National Convention of the Integrated Bar of the Philippines (IBP) reported in: Vincent Cabreza, "Stop paying nuke plant debt, SC justice urges government", *Philippine Daily Inquirer*, 21 April 2005.

rights. Debt is in so many ways an essential part of a larger scheme of economic aggression.

It is imperative to continually assert the premise that the right of people to be free from debt precedes and indeed transcends the details of specific debts. This is because the Philippines' debt problem has reached the point where it not only borrows because it is underdeveloped but it remains underdeveloped precisely because it is forced to keep borrowing with all its adverse effects. This is a situation it shares with hundreds of other Southern countries around the world. More than anything else the corresponding action demanded is to decisively break this cycle of debt and underdevelopment. Relieving the debt burden in its entirety is just one element—albeit a crucial element—and it is also necessary to create conditions in which this problem does not re-emerge. On this aspect of Philippine debt considered in general or in their entirety, the only empirical matter to establish is that the debt has indeed been damaging for society and the economy as a whole.

At the same time it is also useful to consider the extent to which that larger notion of the illegitimacy of Philippine debt can be used to evaluate or assess specific debts. This requires the debt problem also to be appreciated at another level: that of the particular manner in which specific debts may have served, and continue to serve, as instruments of exploitation and plunder. At this level, the issue to highlight is how particular debts are entered into by self-serving capitalists and the state for their benefit at the expense of the Filipino people. However one must be mindful that what is true of the whole debt burden (i.e., that it is antidevelopmental) will not necessarily be the case in the same manner for each and every part—because the whole of the debt burden is more than merely the sum of its parts.

Aside from the larger dimension of the Philippine debt problem, it may be possible to identify specific points of attack on particular loans. The most pertinent aspects and the most productive to highlight are those which relate most closely to how debt is used as an instrument of economic aggression. There are three particularly excessive or brazen aspects according to how they have been used to benefit dominant powers at the expense of the Filipino people; they are not mutually exclusive and indeed often co-exist or overlap in any particular instance of debt.

The first is how there is Philippine debt knowingly given by creditors in gross disregard of the character of the debtor (particularly the state) and the likely misuse of the funds. These include odious debts or loans given to repressive regimes. The most important matters to establish here include, among others, the repressive and undemocratic character of the regime in question and the willful support nonetheless given by creditors. These also include debts ostensibly for developmental projects which, because they were not implemented by a genuinely developmental state, went instead to projects evidently harmful to people or the environment. On this aspect the actual adverse effects of loan-funded projects need to be established. Violations of established project appraisal and evaluation procedures may also be useful although any resort to investigating such possible violations needs to be mindful of how there may be adverse effects even if established procedures have been technically complied with.

The second is that the Philippine debt has been made into an unjustly profitable opportunity for a select few, the costs of which are directly or indirectly borne by the people. These include debt on patently onerous terms and fraudulent debt. These also include debts contracted through transactions imbued with corruption. The unreasonably burdensome character of the loans here needs to be defined and established. It is also frequently the case that such loans push through only with the intervention of highly-placed government officials, and the corrupt action or behavior needs to be established.

Thirdly, the Philippine debt is used to impose economic policy conditions toward creating profitable opportunities for foreign and domestic elites at the expense of the country. This includes multilateral and bilateral loans with explicit policy conditionalities. But this arguably also includes commercial and bondholder debt that, given the dynamics of economic policymaking in the context of the increasing financialization of the global economy, involves implicit conditionalities.[9] The causal link between the debt and the economic policies needs to be established, while mindful that creditor "influence" is exercised in a host of direct and indirect ways. Policy-based loans from the international financial institutions, for instance, have the most explicit conditionalities. Yet even if project-based loans per se do not always have such conditionalities, it may be plausibly argued that they are given in the context of

---

[9] For instance, governments of countries tend to be considered "credit-worthy" if they follow "free market" policies of open trade and investment as well as practice policies of fiscal and monetary restraint. On the other hand, countries with governments that dare to control trade and investment, provide substantial social services and direct financial resources according to development plans, are deemed riskier.

a larger "development assistance" package that in its entirety involves conditionalities regarding policies.

Appreciating debt at this level and in this way certainly makes the issue potentially more practicable. This practicability however varies given the unevenness in terms of actually existing legal and institutional options or avenues for each case. There are, for instance, relatively well-defined domestic laws on graft, corruption and fraud in the Philippines (although many are inapplicable to international contracts). In contrast, there is no provision in domestic law on the crucial issues of odious debts, destructive projects and the imposition of policy conditionalities; hence, these are not straightforwardly expressible in strict legal terms. There is also the fundamental limitation of working within current narrow legal and institutional frameworks that have actually in large part and for so long accommodated illegitimate debts. The well-known difficulties of prosecuting powerful political and economic interests—especially in Third World contexts where they wield so much power—also cannot be underestimated.

Thus defining illegitimate debt in the Philippines or indeed anywhere else cannot be done in a vacuum. Ultimately, the most effective, precise and workable definition is that which will most contribute to advancing the struggle against unjust social and economic systems. In practice the balance that must be struck is between two things. On the one hand, there is the immediate practicability that arises from hewing closely to the framework and language of existing national and international laws. On the other hand, there is the need to continuously assert principles of social justice and in so doing actively challenge the boundaries of prevailing laws and practices.

4. Conclusion and recommendations

The Philippine experience is useful for highlighting the gains to be achieved from working on the basis of a vibrant social and mass movement. At the same time, it highlights some pitfalls in legal struggles. There is the general limitation that the core element of the illegitimacy of debt does not find expression in legal terms. But even if there appear to be some provisions in the 1987 constitution and in international and domestic law that may be used as starting points for voiding loan contracts, these are uneven in their applicability and still subject to interpretation. Unfortunately the interpretation that has been handed down so far has not been favorable. Moreover, the relatively strict requirements of judicial scrutiny can be cumbersome. Even what might be straightforward corruption cases that could be used as the basis for voiding contracts have, in truth, not prospered, likely for "political" reasons.

Based on the foregoing, this paper proposes two distinct but closely related thrusts. The first is to sustain and strengthen the political forces advancing the concept of illegitimate debt; the second, on that basis and without sacrificing momentum, is to expand efforts in more formal legal and institutional realms. Underpinning these both is that a just and lasting solution to the Philippine debt crisis cannot but be comprehensive and go beyond the immediate objective of reducing debt, and all the measures to be taken must retain the focus on the underdevelopment that both creates the conditions for, and is the result of, the debt burden. Thus the efforts need to be innovative in achieving immediate victories and specific gains while retaining that crucial strategic focus.

Social movements have established high standards for the illegitimacy of debt, and this needs to be maintained. This is all the more critical given concrete Philippine conditions where, unfortunately, there are legal precedents that need to be overcome to promote the core concept of "illegitimacy." Indeed, the bias for debts to be considered "legitimate" is heavily reinforced by economic policies that implicitly and explicitly give foreign borrowing and global capital markets special status, and also in a de facto manner, by subjecting claims to the contrary to cumbersome legal processes.

Promoting illegitimate debt as a concept in the Philippines can only be done if this is placed in its proper historical and overall socioeconomic context. In the context of efforts to address the Philippine debt problem it is important to underscore how this cannot take place exclusively or indeed primarily in the legal realm. Pursuing legal avenues and building solid legal cases against instances of illegitimate debt will unarguably advance the overall campaign. However considering the built-in advantages that creditors and pro-debt economic managers have—as clearly seen in the Philippine context—the public pressure and assertion of social movements becomes decisive. The primary motive force of the struggle must take place at the political level and there will be successes in the legal realm only insofar as political gains have already been achieved, consolidated and built up, and to the extent that the parameters of the legal struggle have consequently been modified in favor of the people.

The Philippine government will react depending on the influence of progressive officials and parliamentarians, who in turn draw their strength and direction from civil society groups and social movements. Social movements in themselves greatly increase the room to maneuver vis-à-vis the state in terms of parliamentary work, legislation and lobbying. Official economic policies, including those on debt, ultimately respond according to the prevailing balance of social forces. Indeed, this is the case even with the legal system inasmuch as the boundaries between the application of the law and political power are not always easily determinable.

There is clearly little reason to expect Northern creditors to address illegitimate debt. Financial capitalists and commercial banks have the greatest interest in preserving the debt and collecting as much debt service as possible. The situation is essentially the same with the Paris Club forum of powerful creditor-country governments. The development rhetoric of the international financial institutions (IFIs) of the International Monetary Fund (IMF) and the World Bank potentially provide openings. However the limits to these multilaterals are also evident not just in how they have been intrinsic to worsening Southern debt burdens for so long, but also given the current financial problems they face.

On the other hand, there are international organizations that may potentially be maximized, especially insofar as certain objective conditions exist. The international financial and credit system sustains the debt problem which has adversely impacted on the entire economy. The United Nations (UN) system, in particular, has its potentially meaningful declarations and conventions on economic, social and cultural rights that can be used toward a process of remedying this. The UN Committee on Economic, Social and Cultural Rights (UNESCR) can then be called on to:

- conduct a formal review of the impact on the Filipino people of continued debt servicing and trade and investment liberalization, privatization and deregulation policies, to allow the Philippine government to implement the repayments as imposed by the World Bank, the IMF and the World Trade Organization (WTO);

- evaluate the extent to which these debt policies have supported and/or undermined the capacity of the Philippines to meet its commitments as contained in the International Covenant on Economic, Social and Cultural Rights (ICESCR); and

- evaluate the extent to which the Philippine government has abided by its commitments and obligations to respect, protect and promote the realization of economic, social and cultural rights at the national level.

The International Labour Organization (ILO) Committee of Experts on the Application of Conventions and Recommendations (CEACR) can be called on to conduct a formal review of the Philippine government's compliance with its commitments under ILO conventions. The results of these studies can then be formally submitted to the UN Commission on Human Rights (UNCHR), the UN Economic and Social Council (UNECOSOC) and the General Assembly for appropriate action, including holding the Philippine government and the country's creditors accountable for any violations of economic, social and cultural rights and recommending adequate remedy for the victims. The UN may also be called upon to request the International Court of Justice (ICJ) to render an advisory opinion regarding the legality of Philippine external debt policy, World Bank-IMF conditionalities and creditor demands relative to the ICESCR, conventions of the ILO and other agreements to which the Philippines is a signatory. The ambitious objective is for international recognition of the illegitimacy of debt and, consequently, for an overhaul of how the international financial system treats creditors and deals with these debts.

In none of these do the Filipino people have the luxury of time. Every day that passes of the unresolved debt crisis means continued payments—extremely difficult to recover—and continued suffering. The exact approach cannot be oblivious of how nearly three decades have passed and how every day that passes is unacceptable.

Illegitimacy in practice: Case 4

The Finnish government granted a loan to the State of Costa Rica in the form of an export credit, so that it could buy medical equipment from a Finnish company to supply public hospitals in the country. After fraud and corruption became public and audits were undertaken, it became clear that medical equipment was not bought on the basis of a needs assessment provided by hospitals, but on the basis of existing stock and products of the company. As a result, hospitals in rural areas received highly sophisticated equipment, for which they do not have any use, and technical capacities at staff level to operate them do not exist. Partially, equipment remains in basements, still in its original boxes.

In other words: the general population is today repaying a loan to the Finnish government that had been contracted to buy equipment for public hospitals. In many cases, however, this equipment had not been requested by the hospitals. It does not correspond to genuine needs. And it cannot be used. This is another case of illegitimacy.

From Irresponsible to Responsible Lending: A Swedish Perspective

Sofia Svarfvar

Some cases of illegitimate debt are obvious others are more difficult. The question is, what can be learned for the future? Today people in poor countries still carry the burden of debts because the mechanisms to determine the legitimacy of debt are lacking. At the same time, civil society, including churches, is arguing that clearer and binding social and environmental mechanisms for future lending are needed. We cannot afford another debt crisis. In this paper I scrutinize the ongoing discussion in Sweden. I go on to present the European Network on Debt and Development (EURODAD) initiative to create a charter on responsible lending. Finally, I discuss the need for fair loan contracts and for action by the international community in that direction.

Learning from history

A year ago, I was working with a leaflet for popular education and mobilization toward achieving the United Nations Millennium Development Goals (MDGs). I discussed with the designers how to explain a difficult concept such as illegitimate debt to young people in Sweden. After several discussions, we agreed upon trying to present one of the most obvious cases, loans by the international community to former Philippine dictator Ferdinand Marcos. To further illustrate the madness in the lending process, we showed a picture of Imelda Marcos, the wife of the dictator, saying "Can you phone England—I need forty pairs in lime green." Thereafter, we explained that at the time the World Bank and the International Monetary Fund (IMF) were lending money to the former Philippine President, his wife owned four thousand pairs of shoes and, the money, instead of being invested in schools and hospitals, was used to boost Imelda Marcos' wardrobe.

Another case, more complicated and worthy of examination, is the Swedish bilateral credit to Liberia.

Sweden is to cancel a bilateral debt owed by Liberia that has its roots in export credits. The debt cancellation follows a decision of the Paris Club. After some investigation, we found that these export credits were used for the export of ships to the Liberian coastguard in 1979. At that time, Liberia was on the brink of war. Under today's law, these types of ships used by the coastguard (Type 103) would be classified as war material, but in 1979, they were classified as a civilian export. It can be affirmed that the Swedish official export credit agency acted irresponsibly, but it can also be affirmed that all lending entails risks and that it was impossible to know beforehand what was going to happen in Liberia.

In a letter to the Swedish Minister for Development Cooperation, Rt Rev. Sumoward Harris, bishop of the Lutheran Church of Liberia and the Most Rev. Anders Wejryd, archbishop of the Church of Sweden, call upon the Swedish government to include a clear, public acknowledgement of co-responsibility for the origin of the illegitimate debt when it cancels the Liberian debt and, as a consequence of admitting co-responsibility, not to finance the cancellation of bilateral debt from the overseas development assistance (ODA) budget.[1]

Furthermore, the bishop and archbishop affirmed that such steps would constitute a valuable act of justice for peoples and countries affected by the debts contracted against their interests. An admission of co-responsibility would be an important example for other countries, a confirmation that it is possible to face old mistakes with truth and justice. The bishop and archbishop conclude that this is not only a means of dealing with past bilateral debt, but also of establishing responsible lending and relationships based on transparency and full respect for human rights in the future.

The Democratic Republic of Congo (DRC) also has a bilateral debt to Sweden. The origin is again an export credit, this time to a Swedish company investing in the Inga Shaban energy project during the time of President Mobuto Sese Seko's dictatorship. The project took a very long time to finalize and was associated with fraud and corruption. The African Forum and Network on Debt and Development (AFRODAD) affirms that this is an obvious case of illegitimate debt.[2] Since DRC has not reached the completion point in the Heavily Indebted Poor Countries (HIPC) program, Sweden will not cancel the debt until the Paris Club's final decision. The relevant question to ask the Swedish government is,

---

[1] The letter was signed 23 April 2008, Selayea, Lofa County, Liberia **www.svenskakyrkan.se**

[2] For more information on the Inga-Shaban project see **www.afrodad.org**

if they have the courage to scrutinize these bilateral debts, would they admit possible co-responsibility and consider the lessons of the past when dealing with future official export guarantees?

A different approach for lending in the future

Many civil society organizations assert that the moral issue of co-responsibility is an important step toward establishing a different approach for lending in the future. The Swedish Minister for Development speaking in a radio program on the Liberian case said, "It is our moral responsibility to cancel this debt." However, the Swedish government does not admit the co-responsibility and will finance the debt cancellation from the ODA budget. The difficult task is to learn from history and to develop principles for future lending.

For example, the Swedish Export Credits Guarantee Board (EKN) in 2007 signed a guarantee for 16 billion Swedish kroner (SEK) for the Swedish company Saab's sale of a military radar system to Pakistan, a country where widespread human rights violations occur. There is a great risk that this deal will lead to future unsustainable debt.[3] So, what have we learned? And is Sweden at all willing to learn from the Liberian and DRC cases? It must however be mentioned, that the Swedish government took a small step when it presented a government bill to the parliament which recognizes that "International agreements on debt relief to the poorest countries have created better and necessary conditions for development and must be combined with a bigger responsibility among the loan receivers and the lenders."[4]

The Church of Sweden has welcomed this approach from the government.[5] However, it is unclear whether the Swedish government will advocate clearer criteria for future sustainable lending in an international context. Therefore the Church of Sweden continues to stress the importance of the government recognizing the need for a stronger shared responsibility

---

[3] Johanna Sandahl, ed., Stephen Welch, trans., *Coherence Barometer 2008, Civil Society Organisations Check the Pressure on the Swedish Policy for Global Development*, **www.africagroups.org** (accessed 4 September 2008).

[4] Translated from the Swedish government bill 2007/08:89 Swedish policy for global development **www.regeringen.se**

[5] Church of Sweden's comment to the Swedish policy for global development 16 May 2008 Ks 2008/0371.

among both donors and creditors.[6] Responsible lending is not only about the ability to pay; it must be built on binding contracts and processes that are made available in a transparent way for media, the civil society and the parliament in order to make evaluation and monitoring possible.

Initiatives taken

Internationally, several initiatives on responsible lending have been taken. However, all initiatives are voluntary. Already in 2002 the UN Monterrey Consensus stated that "debtors and creditors must share the responsibility for preventing and resolving unsustainable debt situations."

More recently, the World Bank/IMF agreed in 2006 on a debt-sustainable framework for low-income countries. However EURODAD argues that although the framework takes up the issue of responsible lending, it does not "enter into the qualitative aspects of the loan finance on offer nor propose sanctions for lending beyond so-called prudent limits."[7] Moreover, in 2008 the Organisation for Economic Co-operation and Development (OECD) agreed on voluntary principles and guidelines to promote sustainable practices in the provision of official export credits to low-income countries. The G8 and the Paris Club in 2007 outlined the need for a responsible lending charter that is now discussed within the G20[8].

To contribute to the international debate on responsible lending, EURODAD has in a broad consultation among the civil society and experts in the area, developed a Charter for Responsible Lending.[9] The proposals outlined in the paper are intended to launch further debate at the international level. The EURODAD proposal moves away from institution or sector-specific approaches to dealing with concerns over "responsible lending" and "fair resolution of debt crises" toward internationally-recognized legal standards for responsible financing.

The charter covers the following aspects of a loan contract:

- technical and legal terms and conditions
- protection of human rights and the environment
- public consent and transparency

---

[6] Ibid.

[7] Gail Hurley, EURODAD Charter for Responsible Lending, January 2008 **www.eurodad.org**

[8] Ibid., for more information.

[9] Ibid.

- procurement
- repayment difficulties or disputes

EURODAD argues that all these aspects must be included to ensure that terms and conditions are fair, that the loan contraction process is transparent, that human rights and environments of recipient nations are respected, and repayment difficulties or disputes are resolved fairly and efficiently. Many of the requirements outlined in EURODAD's charter are drawn from international treaties and conventions to which lender and borrower nations are signatories.

Furthermore, the charter produced by EURODAD has been discussed and welcomed on several occasions. For example, in a communiqué from the spring meetings of the World Bank in April 2008, the Commonwealth finance ministers from Cameroon, Ghana, Guyana, Malawi, Mozambique, Sierra Leone, United Republic of Tanzania and Zambia welcomed the charter and urged the international community to carefully consider the proposals in forthcoming international discussions on aid effectiveness.[10]

Conclusion

Ultimately, all lending is about taking risks. But, in this paper, I have confirmed that all lending must be about responsibility and account-ability. The challenge is to avoid future debt crises and to ensure that aid money or money from development institutions is not used for cor-ruption or violations of human rights or to destroy the environment. It is a difficult task in a world where the absence of real democracy is a reality. However, that must not prevent the international community from taking further steps on the issue. The churches have a role to play by moving beyond the economic dimension and taking up an ethical approach which focuses on the moral aspects of international finance. Furthermore, the churches can be a driving force in discussions on responsible financing for development.

Past experience tells us that binding principles and contracts are needed. Looking back, it is clear that many loans are immoral and that both lenders and receiving countries have a responsibility for the misuse of resources. But many cases are tricky ones. Some aspects of the loan

---

[10] www.thecommonwealth.org

process can be clearly defined as irresponsible while in other cases, one can assert that it is impossible to know beforehand that the loan would be diverted and perhaps also violate human rights. The question the Swedish government needs to ask itself is: could the Liberian debt have been avoided within an international framework of responsible lending with fair principles and transparent processes?

All in all, lending processes come down to trust. And to secure that trust, contracts that can be monitored by the public are needed, not least in light of substantial increases in lending to poor countries from new donor countries.

Conclusion: "Not Just Numbers" De-legitimizing Illegitimate Debt

Peter N. Prove and Martin Junge

It is common to hear or read references to the "debt crisis" as if it were over, a matter of historical interest only. But levels of external debt and debt service payment obligations represent an ongoing crisis for many low-income countries, and even some middle-income countries. And especially in low-income countries this has direct consequences for the well-being of their people—in terms of lack of access to education, health services, water, sanitation, housing and other basic public services and social infrastructure.

Developing country debt today stands at USD 2.85 trillion, up from USD 2.24 trillion in 2000 and USD 1.3 trillion in 1990. Developing countries paid out more than USD 540 billion in debt service payments in 2005.[1] Low-income countries continue to pay out USD 100 million each day to creditors, diverting large sums of scarce government revenue to external debt service and away from social welfare and infrastructure investment.

The international community's flagship effort to secure a durable exit from debt crisis—the Heavily Indebted Poor Countries (HIPC) Initiative—has resulted in the cancellation of apparently impressive amounts of external debt for at least some heavily indebted poor countries. But it has failed to achieve the lasting exit from debt crisis that was hoped for. In some cases, countries that have been through the HIPC Initiative process now have higher debt stocks and repayments (and worse social consequences) than before they entered the process.

A total of 23 HIPCs have reached completion point under the HIPC Initiative; 10 are at the decision point, and eight are yet to start the process. In

[1] Letter by 14 NGOs to the UN Secretary-General dated 29 February 2008 regarding the forthcoming International Conference on Financing for Development to review the implementation of the Monterrey Consensus to be held in Doha, Qatar.

total, USD 54 billion in debt relief has been delivered to the 23 post-completion-point countries and USD 18 billion to the decision point countries. But
the World Bank itself estimates 12 post-completion-point countries remain
at a moderate risk of debt distress and two at a high risk.[2]

This is because the international community's current approach to
the resolution of sovereign debt crisis is a very narrow one; it does not
take into account the effects of commodity price fluctuations on debt
sustainability nor the interests of attaining the Millennium Development
Goals (MDGs) by the target date of 2015, let alone issues of corruption,
lack of accountability and injustice.

HIPC Initiative debt relief has also come with strings attached—in
the form of onerous conditionalities going well beyond basic fiduciary
standards into micro-management of the economies of impoverished
nations, and often with very negative effects on basic social welfare in
the countries concerned.

Furthermore, the HIPC Initiative does not fundamentally change the
way sovereign debt lending and borrowing is conducted, so as to ensure
that future loan transactions do not lead straight back into the same abyss
(as has indeed been the case for a number of post-HIPC countries).

The basic thesis and argument of this publication is that a much
broader, more comprehensive, less narrowly economic, more human-
centered approach to the management of sovereign debt transactions
and the resolution of related crises, needs to be adopted. Debt, when
viewed in connection with its direct and indirect consequences for social
and human development, is not just a matter of numbers; it is a matter
of people, their livelihoods, their very lives and their children's future.
It is also a matter of justice, since debt crisis is all too often the result
of immoral, corrupt or grossly negligent actions by actors who have
never been held to account for their deeds, leaving the consequences
to be borne instead by whole populations of people who had nothing to
do with the loan transaction.

Accordingly, the common message from all of the contributors to this
book is that law and ethics must provide the framework for sovereign
debt arrangements, rather than a narrowly economic calculation. It is

---

[2] EURODAD report on the Commonwealth Ministerial Forum on Debt Sustainability, 9 April
2008. See also Heavily Indebted Poor Countries (HIPC) Initiative and Multilateral Debt Relief
Initiative (MDRI) Status of Implementation Report, International Development Association and
International Monetary Fund, 12 September 2008.

time to take sovereign debt out of the isolated confines of economics and into the realm of justice.

Churches are uniquely placed to engage in this debate. The churches are present everywhere—in the cities, towns and villages where real people live out their lives. The churches participate in the daily realities of people all over the world. At the same time, churches are organized in international denominational and ecumenical structures that can convey the experiences and sufferings of people at the grassroots into the highest ivory towers of international economic policy discourse. In short, churches are simultaneously both local and global, both horizontally widespread and vertically integrated.

The notion of "communio" informs our thinking in this context. As Christians, we understand ourselves to be all members of the same body of Christ and to share in the pain of any other part of the body. Accordingly, our interests cannot be defined in narrow national terms. The body of Christ recognizes no geographic, national, racial, ethnic, cultural, linguistic or other boundaries.

As churches, we are motivated by faith commitments to the common God-given dignity of every human being and by our diaconic calling. We are impelled by a pastoral concern for the people to whom we minister and whose sufferings we witness and share. Our ethical base refuses to accept impunity for those whose actions knowingly and negligently cause that suffering. And as members of the global body of Christ, we have the vocation of global citizenship, in which national interests cannot prevail over the common interests of humanity and which demands legitimate and effective instruments of global governance. Illegitimate debt and its social consequences is a challenge to the churches and their ministries—a challenge which cannot be left unanswered.

We argue that, legally and ethically, external debt should be examined first and foremost from the perspective of "legitimacy" and not merely from the perspective of "sustainability." Our sense of justice demands that a debt determined to be "illegitimate" should not be repaid, even if from a strictly economic point of view the debtor country can afford to repay it (albeit at heavy cost to the country's capacity to provide basic social services to its people).

Illegitimacy of sovereign debts may derive from different sources and factors. The political circumstances and context in which the debt was contracted may impugn its legitimacy, as in the case of so-called "dictator's debt," where loans are made to governments that are well-known to lack democratic credentials and to be oppressing their own people. Loans may also be considered illegitimate for lack of democratic mandate if they have effectively been forced on the people of a debtor country by the diktat of international financial institutions. Unduly onerous and oppressive loan conditions may also bring the legitimacy of the debts that derive from them into question. Issues of legitimacy may also be raised where the loan has an improper purpose, or where it was not applied for the benefit of the public. Corruption or other illegal behavior on the part of either creditor or borrower may render illegitimate a loan's subsequent enforcement upon populations that had no part in the transaction. And an overall debt burden that prevents a country from making adequate progress toward internationally agreed development goals (in particular the MDGs) may arguably be regarded as illegitimate for that reason—thereby subsuming the issue of sustainability.

Though based in part upon the established legal doctrine of "odious debt," the concept of illegitimate debt is fundamentally a political matter, dependent upon political action for its legal and administrative operationalization.

Some key political actions taken in this direction are described in the contributions to this book. The Norwegian government's acknowledgement of its own responsibility in the case of the debts resulting for the Norwegian ship export campaign was a genuine breakthrough in terms of applying an ethical criterion to a creditor government's own actions. The Government of Ecuador's initiative to establish a commission to investigate the legitimacy of Ecuador's external debts was the first occasion on which such a process had been based on a formal political mandate. These initiatives are landmarks on the path toward a new multilateral consensus on dealing with debt in which ethics and justice prevail over economic calculus.

But unless these landmarks are followed, the path leads nowhere. The challenge now is to have the governments of more creditor countries follow Norway's example in recognizing their own responsibility for specific improper debts and to have the governments of more debtor countries follow Ecuador's example in auditing their debt portfolios from the perspective of legitimacy. This will clearly need to be a key advocacy priority for non-governmental organizations and civil society networks in relevant countries in the next period.

One important civil society initiative concerning creditor co-responsibility is the EURODAD Charter on Responsible Lending, which urges both lenders and borrowers to recognize that they share responsibility for ensuring long term future debt sustainability. The charter aims to move the current discourse on debt sustainability beyond simply trying to ensure that borrowers are not extended loans they may be unable to repay in the future. It aims to promote a discourse on sovereign debt that includes not just an assessment of the economic situation of the borrower but fair terms and conditions, respect for human rights and the environment, greater transparency, parliamentary and citizen participation in the loan contracting process, and mechanisms for the independent, predictable and fair resolution of repayment difficulties and disputes. The proposed Charter was referred to favorably by the Commonwealth Ministerial Debt Sustainability Forum at its meeting in April 2008. This provides useful impetus to this instrument for advancing the case for creditor co-responsibility in sovereign lending.

A number of current inter-governmental/multilateral processes provide opportunities for articulating these issues and advancing a response. At the time that this publication is issued, the process for reviewing the follow-up to and implementation of the International Conference on Financing for Development will be nearing its climax. The original conference, held in Monterrey, Mexico, in March 2002, was unique in establishing a framework for a holistic consideration of all sources for financing development. The Monterrey Consensus noted that "External debt relief can play a key role in liberating resources that can then be directed toward activities consistent with attaining sustainable growth and development,"[3] and expressed commitment to comprehensively addressing the debt problems of developing countries.

The International Conference to Review the Implementation of the Monterrey Consensus on Financing for Development, which takes place in Doha, Qatar, on 29 November–2 December 2008, is intended to assess progress made, reaffirm goals and commitments and share best practices and lessons learned. It should also indentify obstacles and constraints encountered, actions and initiatives to overcome them, important measures for further implementation, as well as new challenges and emerging issues in meeting the challenge of financing for development. Accordingly, the Doha Review Conference will, inter alia, be a key international opportunity for examining progress (or the lack

---

[3] United Nations, "Monterrey Consensus of the International Conference on Financing for Development," Monterrey, 2003, p. 4, para. 48, **www.un.org**

thereof) in fulfilling the commitment to comprehensively addressing the debt problems of developing countries.

Given its focus on the objective of development, the Doha Review Conference will also be a forum in which the argument can be forcefully made for giving the objective of reaching the Millennium Development Goals equal weight with economic performance indicators in decision-making on sovereign debt relief and the allocation of compensatory finance. Indeed, the Monterrey Consensus itself urged that "Future reviews of debt sustainability should also bear in mind the impact of debt relief on progress toward attainment of development goals contained in the Millennium Declaration."[4]

As we move further beyond the halfway mark in the timeline for attainment of the MDGs, it is increasingly apparent that progress toward those goals is at best patchy and that many of the goals will not—on current trends—be met. Some "post-HIPC" countries, like Bolivia, are among the furthest behind in achieving the MDGs. If the international community is serious about reaching the MDGs globally by 2015 much more will have to be done, at the very least, to remove the obstacles in the path of the least developed countries. Chief among these obstacles is the continuing debt crisis. Indeed, enforcing these debt obligations upon the people of least developed countries while at the same time declaring commitment to the MDGs may raise questions of legitimacy as well as of morality.

Since the Monterrey Consensus was adopted there has been a growing legal and political interest in the doctrine of "odious debt" and the related concept of "illegitimate debt." Certainly this is reflected in the actions taken by the governments of Norway and Ecuador, but it is also evident in the cancellation of Iraq's sovereign debts, the political and legal arguments for which included a focus on the odiousness of the previous Iraqi government. It is also reflected in the recent publication of papers on the topic of odious or illegitimate debt by the United Nations Conference on Trade and Development (UNCTAD) and the World Bank. One may hope that the debate provoked by these papers may yet lead to specific policy shifts in relevant international economic forums.

Another policy stream that may converge with the others mentioned above is that of international human rights. The UN Commission on Human Rights—now succeeded by the UN Human Rights Council—has had a growing engagement in promoting the relevance of human rights

---

[4] Ibid., para. 49.

in economic policy discourse. This has been especially the case with regard to external debt and international trade policy. One of the "special procedures" of the UN Human Rights Council is the mandate of "Independent Expert on the effects of economic reform policies and foreign debt and other related international financial obligations of States on the full enjoyment of all human rights, particularly economic, social and cultural rights" (Dr Cephas Lumina of Zambia has recently been appointed to this mandate). In addition, the UN Committee on Economic, Social and Cultural Rights (the independent expert body responsible for monitoring compliance with the International Covenant on Economic, Social and Cultural Rights) has frequently expressed concern about the impact of external debt on the capacity of low income countries to promote the progressive realization of the rights enshrined in the Covenant. It should also be noted that Art. 2(1) of the Covenant commits States Parties to cooperating internationally for the realization of economic, social and cultural rights, and that this has obvious implications for the conduct of creditor states with regard to sovereign debt transactions.

Human rights law potentially has a great deal to add to the further articulation and operationalization of the concept of illegitimate debt. It is an international legal and policy framework that is based on very deep ethical foundations and broad understandings of the essential requirements of human dignity. It addresses economic, social and cultural rights as well as civil and political rights, and therefore has direct implications for economic policy at the national and international levels. It is also a body of international law that is well-recognized in state practice, and in some respects has acquired the status of customary international law. It is also expressed in a number of widely-ratified international treaties. It brings both legal and moral force together in the one set of principles and instruments. In our understanding, the proper application of international human rights law in the context of sovereign debt transactions would require the cancellation of illegitimate debts.

Out of these many streams, we believe that the river flows inexorably toward an approach to external debt that is not constrained by the boundaries of one discipline, but rather takes into account all the circumstances and consequences of sovereign debt transactions. In this as in many other areas of economic policy, human beings and communities must be recognized as the central and indeed only purpose to be served.

As we write, the world is in the midst of an economic crisis, with commodity prices rising everywhere, inflation resurgent, banks failing and recession threatening. In the midst of this crisis, the role and responsibility of unaccountable and corrupt elites is increasingly exposed. Every crisis is also an opportunity. The present crisis presents an opportunity for re-drawing some of the architecture of international economic governance—and for insisting that external debt and its effects are not just numbers.

Contributors

Kjetil G. Abildsnes, SLUG (Norwegian Jubilee Campaign)

Rev. Dr Walter Altmann, president of the Evangelical Church of the Lutheran Confession in Brazil (IECLB) and moderator of the World Council of Churches (WCC) Central Committee

Bishop Dr Joseph P. Bvumbwe, head of the Evangelical Lutheran Church in Malawi, chairperson of the LWF National Committee in Malawi

Rev. Ángel F. Furlan, coordinator of the LWF program on Illegitimate Debt located in Buenos Aires, Argentina

Joseph Hanlon, senior lecturer in development and conflict resolution, International Development Centre, Open University, Milton Keynes, UK

Rev. Martin Junge, area secretary for Latin America & the Caribbean, LWF Department for Mission and Development

Jürgen Kaiser, political coordinator, erlassjahr.de

Rev. Dr Kjell Nordstokke, director of the LWF Department for Mission and Development

Alejandro Olmos, researcher, historian and expert in international public law, Argentina

Peter N. Prove, assistant to the general secretary for International Affairs and Human Rights at the LWF

Rev. Dr Gloria Rojas, moderator of the Latin American Church Leadership Conference and president of the Evangelical Lutheran Church in Chile

Rev. Juan Pedro Schaad, coordinator of the LWF program on
  Illegitimate Debt located in Buenos Aires, Argentina

Sofia Svarfvar, policy adviser for global economy at Church of
  Sweden